DESIGN SPACE

A Beginners Guide with Original Project Ideas.

Tip, Tricks, Techniques and Accessories on
How to Start Cricut Machine Maker.

Learn How to Use Tool and Function.

Matt Space

This document is geared towards providing exact and reliable information with regards to the topic and issue covered. The publication is sold with the idea that the publisher is not required to render accounting, officially permitted, or otherwise, qualified services. If advice is necessary, legal or professional, a practiced individual in the profession should be ordered.

From a declaration of principles which was accepted and approved equally by a committee of the American Bar Association and a Committee of Publisher And Associations.

In no way is it legal to reproduce, duplicate, or transmit any part of this document in either electronic means or in printed format. Recording of this publication is strictly prohibited and any storage of this document is not allowed unless with written permission from the publisher. All rights reserved.

The information provided herein is stated to be truthful and consistent, in that any liability, in terms of inattention or otherwise, by any usage or abuse of any policies, processes, or directions contained within is the solitary and utter responsibility of the recipient reader. Under no circumstances will any legal responsibility or blame be held against the publisher for any reparation, damages, or monetary loss due to the information herein, either directly or indirectly.

Respective authors own all copyrights not held by the publisher.

The information herein is offered for informational purposes solely, and is universal as so. The presentation of the information is without contract or any type of guarantee assurance.

The trademarks that are used are without any consent, and the publication of the trademark is without permission or backing by the trademark owner. All trademarks and brands within this book are for clarifying purposes only and are the owned by the owners themselves, not affiliated with this document.

Table of Contents

INTRODUCTION 7

BASICS OF CRICUT MACHINE 10

TIPS AND TRICKS FOR CRICUT MACHINE AND CRICUT MAKER 15

WHAT IS CRICUT DESIGN SPACE AND WHY YOU SHOULD START 27

HOW TO START USING THE CRICUT MACHINE EVEN WITH NO EXPERIENCE 37

DESIGN SPACE SOFTWARE SECRETS 55

SUREFIRE WAYS TO MAKE MONEY WITH YOUR CRICUT 72

HOW TO REALIZE AND EDIT CRICUT PROJECT IDEAS 81

CRICUT MACHINE TROUBLESHOOTING TIPS 102

PRACTICAL EXAMPLES AND STRATEGIES FOR EVERY KIND OF PROJECT 156

ALL YOU NEED TO KNOW TO BECOME A PROFESSIONAL 182

HOW TO TURN YOUR CREATIVITY INTO AN AMAZING BUSINESS 199

STEP BY STEP INSTRUCTIONS TO CUT PDF SEWING PATTERNS ON THE CRICUT MAKER 211

CONCLUSION 260

INTRODUCTION

Is it accurate to say that you are attempting to get the hang of everything about Cricut Design Space and you don't realize where to begin?

Learning another pastime or aptitude can be scary from the start. I get it, now and then we don't realize where to begin because there's such a great amount of data out there and it's simply overpowering.

For me, the ideal approach to learn and ace Cricut Design Space is from the earliest starting point!

When you have a reasonable idea of what each symbol and board is for, then you can genuinely dive in and begin investigating further and further.

Once in a while, we rush to bounce from undertaking to extend – Hey That's alright as well! BTDT – But I feel that knowing your work zone will assist you with taking your imagination in an unheard of level.

Many creating devotees have become hopelessly enamored with their own electronic bite the dust cut machine, the Cricut. Another expansion to the officially prominent item is the advancement of a product program made only for Cricut clients.

Cricut Design Space is a PC programming system made by Provocraft, the designers of the Cricut machine. While the machine itself enables the client to cut different shapes and textual styles in a fury of sizes, the Cricut Design Space takes it to an unheard of level. Just interface the Cricut to the PC through a USB port, introduce the product, and release a totally different element of making.

The principle advantage of the Cricut Design Space is the capacity for clients to weld, or associate letters together to frame a solitary cutting. Gone are the times of sticking each letter each one in turn. Presently letters, expressions, and shapes can be welded together before cutting, making it quicker and simpler than any time in recent memory to add cuttings to ventures.

Another advantage of the Cricut Design Space is that the shapes and letters can be controlled widely before cutting. Clients are never again restricted to just modifying the size, yet would now be able to change the shape properties to all the more likely help their general design. Each picture can be extended, inclined, and turned to get the accurate look the crafter is requiring.

While the Cricut Design Space has many benefits, my undisputed top choice is the capacity to fuse pictures from different cartridges into one design. The client would now be able to design with all the cartridge choices without a moment's delay as opposed to being constrained to cutting with one cartridge at any given moment.

Progressed and ultra-inventive clients have made remarkable tasks by consolidating a few different cartridges into one mind blowing cutting.

The Cricut Design Space is, as I would like to think, a need for each Cricut proprietor. While there is an expectation to absorb information to it when it is comprehended, the imaginative alternatives are completely boundless. The Cricut and the Design Space have turned into an absolute necessity have asset for each scrapbooker and card creator today.

BASICS OF CRICUT MACHINE

Before you start working with your Cricut Machine, ensure you get familiar with the nuts and bolts first. I have connections to posts where I reveal to you how to begin with Design Space, why I cherish my Cricut Maker, in addition to certain materials you can attempt.

There are such a significant number of potential outcomes you can make with your Cricut Machine, however none of that will matter if you don't have a clue how to utilize their product.

I have been working with the product for over a year and have taken in the intricate details. Presently you don't need to scour the interwebs for assets because all that you have to ace Cricut Design Space will in all likelihood be in this rundown!

Clearly you'll require a Cricut machine, however I've recorded a portion of my most loved Cricut supplies and materials in the accompanying posts!

Cricut Machine Tips

When I previously got my Cricut Explore Air, I was so scared.

It sat in the crate for quite a long time, because I simply didn't have the foggiest idea where to begin.

All things considered, those were squandered months, because it has transformed into one of my preferred diversions.

I'm not one of those individuals who has each task turn out impeccably – indeed, many end in tears or simply being finished rashly because it simply does not merit wrapping up!

In any case, I have taken in much throughout the years, and I trust that this post will help those of you who are simply beginning and need a smidgen of additional assistance.

What Machine Should I get?

If you are reading this, you likely as of now have a machine – yet you may likewise be attempting to choose which one is best for you.

There are a huge amount of different Cricut machines out there, however the two lines that they still effectively update and advance are the Explore Air line and the Cricut Maker.

I am blessed to possess the Air, Air 2 and Maker, and truly, they are on the whole astounding machines. There are things I like about the Air more than the Maker, yet by and large, I like the power and potential outcomes of the Maker.

Transfer your own image.

You can transfer your very own structure, textual style, and thoughts right to your own plan space. I want to utilize

Picmonkey online because it is free thus simple to utilize. Obviously, you can utilize other structure applications that are further developed, yet if you need to take a stab at some plan this is a great spot to begin.

If you need you would prefer not to make your own picture you can utilize the Cricut picture library and locate the ideal picture for your venture. Cricut offers in excess of 60,000 pictures beginning at only 99 pennies.

Compose with your Cricut Explore air 2. I love this feature.

If you have some extravagant solicitations or even a statement or saying you need to make as a presentation in your home or a gift this is highlight is astounding thus one of a kind to Cricut.

Keeping your mats clean.

Your machine will accompany a cutting mat. Ensure you are clearing your each time you use it and re-covering it with the plastic spread that accompanies the tangle. If you need giving it a little lift you can wash it with water and gentle cleanser, forgetting about it to dry. Another alternate way for a tangle that is never again clingy is to utilize painters tap or washi tape to hold your venture set up as the machine cuts.

Use Cricut.com as an asset for all that you need. There are such a significant number of youtube recordings and venture tips accessible right on the site. If you are feeling like you need significantly more help scan for instructional exercises on Pinterest or google and you will discover a pack.

Keep your blades sharp.

It is a smart thought to keep your cutting edges independent and utilized for each different material that it is fitting for. A smart thought may be to check every sharp edge by class utilizing washi tape or fingernail clean.

Cricut Access.

You have likely found before long that the vast majority of the alternatives accessible on Cricut will cost a couple of dollars to utilize. If you intend to utilize different textual styles and like to take a shot at a couple of undertakings a month you will need to consider buying in to Cricut Access. I found that just have a couple of textual style decisions I was at that point at the expense of the exceptional access. One thing to remember is that when you buy in to this administration the majority of your buys will remain in your record. No compelling reason to stress over cartridges! If you drop your membership you will lose access to these highlights.

If you discover a textual style that you cherish and utilize constantly, you may simply need to purchase that text style and move along not agonizing over the membership, the decision is up to you.

Practice Cut.

The new Cricut Air 2 machine is more intelligent than any time in recent memory and can change in accordance with your needs with the spot of the handle. While this is mind blowing, it doesn't represent client blunder. Ha! I needed to rehearse a couple of times just to make sense of what direction I should lay the vinyl or the texture of the venture I am taking a shot at. If you are utilizing a constrained measure of a material in your gathering you might need to have some piece materials that are a similar thickness so you can have challenges and not sob late into the night that night.

TIPS AND TRICKS FOR CRICUT MACHINE AND CRICUT MAKER

These are marvelous cutting machines. They can accomplish such huge numbers of things, and the venture potential outcomes truly are perpetual! Notwithstanding, "Where do I start!?" was often heard all through my home on the day I got my first Cricut machine, the Explore Air 2.

All things considered, I endure those first days and need to impart to you 25 hints and deceives for beginning with your new Cricut machine. Nowadays I'm for the most part utilizing the Cricut Maker, however the vast majority of these tips are applicable to the two models!

Alright, so a portion of these tips and deceives are VERY essential, and are for the total novice to Cricut machines. In any case, ensure you filter through the entire rundown because we guarantee there's a tip or stunt with your name on it!

1. Buy in To Cricut Access

If you truly need to benefit from having a Cricut Explore Air 2, then we prescribe buying in to Cricut Access. You can pay a month to month expense of around $10, or a yearly charge which works out to be somewhat less expensive every month.

Cricut Access gives you access to 30,000+ pictures, 1000's of tasks and more than 370 textual styles. If you will be utilizing your Cricut a ton, then this will spare you a great deal of cash than if you were to purchase each extend and picture independently.

Besides it's to a lesser degree a problem to pay a level rate than to stress over how a lot of cash you're really spending on ventures! It includes! Get your full value out of your Cricut by making the magnificent Design Space ventures. Get familiar with Cricut Access here.

2. De-tack Your Cutting Mat

De-tack your Cricut cutting mat a bit!

The Explore Air 2 more often than not accompanies the green standard cutting mat, while the Maker as a rule accompanies the blue light hold tangle. You place your materials onto the tangle before placing it into the machine.

The green cutting mat is really clingy when shiny new! After you strip the plastic spread off, you can put a spotless, dry shirt over the tangle so as to prime it for your first venture. It's extremely difficult to get the cardstock off, regardless of whether you have every one of the instruments, when it's at its full tenacity! It's anything but difficult to harm the venture while attempting to get it off.

You shouldn't have this issue with the blue light grasp tangle, so you could likewise buy that for your paper and card extends rather than de-attaching the green tangle.

Likewise, look at the full scope of Cricut mats for different materials.

3. Keep Your Cutting Mat Covers

The cutting mats accompany a plastic shield covering them. This can be pulled off and set back on effectively. We kept our spread and set it back on our tangle when we are done with it – it keeps the tangle spotless and clingy longer!

4. Cleaning The Cricut Cutting Mat

Each now and again (if not each time you use it), give your cutting mat a wipe over with some infant wipes. The non-liquor water wipes without scent are ideal. This will keep it free from structure up with cardstock and vinyl buildup from cutting, and all the standard family unit residue and build up coasting about.

5. Get The Right Tools

Ensure you have the Cricut Tool Set! It contains a weeding device, a scrubber, tweezers, a spatula and scissors. It is particularly useful to have the weeding device if you are anticipating cutting either cement vinyl or warmth move vinyl.

6. Request The Cricut Scoring Stylus

Such a large number of the card undertakings expect you to have the scoring stylus. I didn't structure one with my machine from the start, thus had a difficult sit tight for it to land before I could go on to some better ventures. If you purchased your machine as a component of a group, it might have the scoring stylus included, so twofold watch that.

7. Start With The Sample Project

When your machine shows up, start with the example venture. The Explore Air 2 accompanies test cardstock for you to make your first card. You will get the negligible measure of materials to do this unparalleled card. Instead of attempting to accomplish something significant and extravagant, simply start here to discover how things work – programming and equipment astute.

8. Test Cuts

When doing your very own undertakings it very well may be savvy to do a test cut before accomplishing the entire thing. If the sharp edge is set too low it will demolish your cutting mat. If it's too high it might just slice somewhat through your vinyl, cardstock, and so forth and ruin your materials. Doing a test cut may include requesting that your machine cut a little circle. Watch that the setting is correct and make changes if vital.

9. Supplant Pen Lids After Use

It's so natural to overlook your pen is in the machine after you've completed a task. I generally become involved with what I'm doing and overlook it's hanging out in there! Be that as it may, it is critical to get the top on it asap after you've completed the process of utilizing it with the goal that it doesn't dry out. They are too costly to even consider wasting. The cool thing about the Design Space undertakings is that it often prompts you to return the cover on!

10. Connection Your Old Cricut Cartridges To Your Design Space Account

Remember to attach any old cartridges you may have had from a past machine to your new record. This is a genuinely basic methodology, as demonstrated as follows. Every cartridge must be connected once, so if you're taking a gander at getting some second hand, affirm this hasn't occurred at this point!

11. Getting Materials Off The Cutting Mat

Other than utilizing the fitting instruments to evacuate your cardstock or vinyl (eg. Cricut Iron On) from the cutting mat, there is another stunt to getting it off. Rather than stripping your task from the tangle, which can bring about twisting (or absolute ravaging), strip the tangle away from your undertaking. Curve the tangle away from the card instead of a different way.

It might flip around the tangle and curve one corner to lift the cardstock. You would then be able to slip the spatula instrument under to expel your task. Before I had the correct instruments I was utilizing a Visa to get card off the tangle, which I thought would be fine, yet it harmed the glue on the tangle.

12. Request The Deep Cut Blade

There's nothing more regrettable than setting your heart upon a task and afterward finding you don't have the correct instruments! The profound slice cutting edge enables you to slice through thicker card, calfskin, chipboard and then some. This cutting edge is perfect with the Explore Air 2. It is essential to get the cutting edge, yet the sharp edge lodging too. Try not to hold up till you need it, request it now!

13. Set aside Cash By Using Free SVG documents

You don't just need to utilize plans from the Design Space store. You can either make your own SVG documents, or utilize other free SVG records which can be discovered everywhere throughout the web. We have a rundown of sites with free SVG records.

14. Different Pens Work In The Explore Air 2 Too

There are different pens that you can use in the Explore Air 2 (and any machine with the frill connector) other than the Cricut pens. These incorporate, yet are not constrained to, Sharpie Pens and American Craft Pens. Cricut pens do appear to be awesome quality however, my pens in every case keep going quite a while.

15. Burden Mat Correctly

Ensure your tangle is appropriately stacked before you start cutting. It needs to sneak by the rollers. Your machine will probably simply begin cutting before the highest point of the lattice on the tangle or not in any manner if it hasn't been stacked right.

16. Utilizing Free Fonts For Your Projects

There are such a large number of free text style destinations for you to begin utilizing! See here for a rundown of thousands of free text styles. You essentially download the textual style, introduce it to your PC and it will show up in your Cricut Design Space (see next tip).

17. Introducing Fonts Into Design Space

Subsequent to introducing a text style to your PC, you may need to sign out and over into Cricut Design Space before your new textual style will appear there. You may even need to restart your PC for it to appear (mine wouldn't appear without restarting my PC). For more data read how to introduce textual styles in Cricut Design Space.

18. Supplanting Blades

Like everything, Cricut edges wear out. When the cuts are never again so smooth and powerful it's the ideal opportunity for a change. Different signs that you need another sharp edge include: tearing card or vinyl lifting or pulling vinyl off the support sheet not carving right through (ensure your cut setting is right also)

You can buy new cutting edges on Amazon or read this Cricut Blade Guide.

19. When Your Mat Loses Its Stick

Cleaning your tangle is one approach to help get somewhat more life out of your cutting mat. Yet, if it's past that, and you have not requested another cutting mat yet, you can tape down your card or vinyl to hold it set up. Clearly, you would prefer not to tape over a region that is waiting be chopped, however down a few sides ought to carry out the responsibility. A medium tack painters tape is appropriate for this assignment, and ought not harm your cardstock.

20. Cricut's Custom Cut Settings

The Explore Air 2 accompanies 7 preset choices on the dial:

Paper

Vinyl

Iron-on

Light cardstock

Cardstock

Fortified texture

Notice board

If the material you are cutting isn't on this rundown, there is a custom choice which you can choose on the dial. Go into

Design Space, select your task and snap 'Make It'. You will then have the option to choose your material from a drop down menu.

On the other hand you can make another custom material. You can discover more data about this over at Cricut's site.

21. Different Blades For Different Materials

A few people depend on utilizing separate sharp edges for cutting every material. For instance, having one cutting edge that you use for cardstock, and another that you use for vinyl. This is because the different materials will wear differently on your sharp edges. Cutting vinyl is simpler on the sharp edge than slicing through card.

Having a devoted cutting edge for vinyl implies it will consistently be prepared and sharp, instead of having one edge for everything that rapidly goes obtuse and afterward lifts up your valuable vinyl! We haven't attempted this stunt ourselves, however will do as such and report back our discoveries!

22. Remember To Mirror Your Image When Cutting HTV

If you are cutting warmth move vinyl with your Cricut, you should reflect your plan! After you select 'Make It' there is a choice to reflect your plan (as observed beneath), and you should choose this choice for every individual tangle!

23. Spot Your HTV On The Cutting Mat The Right Way Up

So as to cut warmth move vinyl you should put your vinyl gleaming side down on the cutting mat. Along these lines the transporter sheet is underneath and the dull vinyl side is on top. It's difficult to see which side the bearer sheet is on, so simply recollect sparkly side down and you'll be fine!

24. Use Weeding Boxes For Small and Intricate Designs

If you are removing a little or unpredictable structure, or you are removing a variety of plans on one sheet of vinyl, it can utilize weeding boxes.

Simply utilize the square apparatus in Cricut Design Space to put a case around your structure and gathering the two components together. Open the shape in the base left corner to control it into a square shape.

This makes weeding a lot simpler than weeding a few structures without a moment's delay on the one sheet of vinyl, and a lot simpler than attempting to see where your plans are and removing them independently with scissors.

25. Make sure To Set The Dial

This tip appears to be an easy decision, however how frequently have I neglected to change the material setting?! It's such a simple thing to overlook – particularly when you have at last completed your plan and truly need to get cutting! Interestingly, Cricut Design Space really discloses to you what material the dial is set to when you are going to remove a structure – however it is not entirely obvious that as well!

Spare yourself the slip-up of slicing directly through to your cutting mat, or not absolutely through your cardstock – consistently check your dial!

... And now we have a reward tip!

26! Keep up A Supply Of Materials

As we referenced before, it's a torment when you need to begin an undertaking and you don't have the correct apparatuses. For instance, we've been in the situation of being without the scoring stylus, without the correct pen for an undertaking, and without a profound cut sharp edge. In any case, the other issue is when you need to do a venture and you've come up short on glue vinyl, HTV or cardstock!

WHAT IS CRICUT DESIGN SPACE AND WHY YOU SHOULD START

Cricut Design Space is the online stage that Cricut designed to be utilized with their more up to date machines.

It's not programming – you download a module on your PC (or the application on your table/telephone), and after that, you can design however much you might want.

You can utilize designs and pictures that are now transferred into Design Space, or you can transfer your own!

Cricut Design Space is 100% free. You do need to make a record; however, if you would prefer not to, you don't need to spend a penny.

Cricut Design Space is an online programming program that enables you to interface with your cutting machines by means of USB or bluetooth. It's the way you make the majority of the wonderful designs that will wind up on your tasks, shirts, cushions, espresso cups, and the sky is the limit from there!

It's likewise preloaded with heaps of prepared to make extends that are made by Cricut and different clients. If you don't think you'd be any great at beginning without any preparation, or possibly you do not have the tolerance to do this, there is still bounty you can do with your Cricut through Cricut Design Space.

As an option in contrast to making your own designs or getting them from Cricut, I regularly shop at Etsy (simply scan what you're searching for with SVG toward the end) and afterward "play with" my designs. You can perceive how I do this in the video underneath, which additionally incorporates a fast stroll through presentation of Design Space:

While they have some free pictures and textual styles incorporated with the program, there are ones that you can pay cash for. You can likewise pursue a Cricut Access Plan, which will give you access to a great many pictures and textual styles.

Be that as it may, you can introduce your own textual styles onto your PC and transfer pictures to Design Space (that you've made, found for nothing, or obtained without anyone else).

Cricut Design Space is an online program, so you don't download it onto your PC.

Nonetheless, you should download some modules, which should auto popup and brief you to download when you experience the underlying procedure.

If you are needing to download Cricut Design Space onto your iPhone or iPad, then you will simply need to go to the Apple App Store, scan for "Design Space," and it ought to be the primary alternative to spring up. Download it like you regularly would.

Any undertaking that you make in Design Space can be spared to the Cloud. You simply need to ensure you spare your venture – that catch is in the upper right hand corner.

This enables you to see your task on any gadget where you are signed in.

Nonetheless, if you are dealing with an iPhone or an iPad, you have the choice to spare it just to your gadget. I would, for the most part, consistently propose sparing it to the Cloud, however!

You can utilize Design Space on Mac PCs, PC PCs, and iOS gadgets.

Your PC must run a Windows or Mac working framework, and hence, Google Chromebooks CANNOT be utilized, as they keep running on a Google OS.

Once in a while when you go to cut your design, it will stop you before you at the tangle see page and state you have to pay.

You may have incidentally included a picture that requires installment – you can return to your canvas and check each picture to check whether there is a dollar sign beside it (or check whether the text style you chose has a dollar sign. Remember that regardless of whether you have Cricut Access, you don't approach ALL the pictures and textual styles).

If you chose a venture from Design Space, it might have incorporated a picture or textual style that is paid. When you take a gander at the task guidelines, it should let you know if it is free or not.

I see this inquiry all the time in Design Space, and it very well may be so disappointing! Frequently, Design Space is down when they are making refreshes.

Some of the time, they will convey an email when they anticipate a blackout. However, I don't generally observe this.

If it's down, I would propose not reaching their client backing and simply be quiet. You can likewise attempt another program or clear your program store, just to ensure it is anything but an issue on your end.

Cutting is one of my preferred highlights in Cricut Design Space! I cherish removing text styles and pictures in different designs.

Yet, now and then it won't work. If you are observing this to be an issue, here are a couple of thoughts:

– Make sure the picture/text style you are removing of (so that is over another picture) is totally inside the other picture. If a bit of it is standing out, it won't cut.

– Make sure everything is chosen.

– Keep as a main priority that when you cut it, you will have two layers to expel from the picture – the first picture/text style that you cut, just as the cut

For what reason isn't Print and Cut working?

I won't jump a lot into Print and Cut, as it is a monster all alone.

Notwithstanding, the most compelling motivation why I see individuals experiencing difficulty with Print and Cut is that they didn't smooth their pictures! Before you go to print and cut, ensure you select all and press straighten.

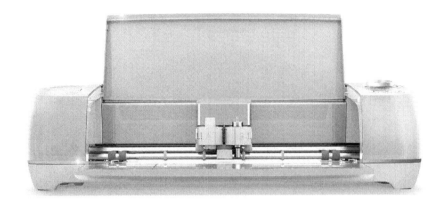

For what reason Can't I Open Cricut Design Space?

Regularly you will get a blunder or a white screen with Design Space if you don't have the most as of late refreshed module.

If you get a clear page, take a stab at invigorating the page to check whether the module update shows up. Try not to move far from this page when it's refreshing, or it will turn white.

Cartridge

Designs are produced using parts put away on cartridges. Every cartridge accompanies a console overlay and guidance booklet. The plastic console overlay demonstrates key determinations for that cartridge as it were. Anyway as of late Provo Craft has discharged an "All inclusive Overlay" that is perfect with all cartridges discharged after August 1, 2013. The motivation behind the all-inclusive overlay is to simplify the way toward slicing by just learning one console overlay as opposed to learning the overlay for every individual cartridge. Designs can be removed on a PC with the Cricut Design Studio programming, on a USB associated Gypsy machine, or can be legitimately inputted on the Cricut machine utilizing the console overlay. There are two kinds of cartridges shape and textual style. Every cartridge has an assortment of imaginative highlights which can take into consideration several different cuts from only one cartridge. There are as of now more than 275 cartridges that are accessible (independently from the machine), containing textual styles and shapes, with new ones included monthly. While a few cartridges are conventional in substance, Cricut has permitting concurrences with Disney, Pixar, Nickelodeon, Sesame Street, DC Comics and Hello Kitty. The Cricut line has a scope of costs, yet the cartridges are compatible, despite the fact that not all alternatives on a cartridge might be accessible with the littler machines. All cartridges work just with Cricut programming, must be enrolled to a solitary client for use and can't be sold or given away. A cartridge obtained for a suspended machine is probably going to wind up futile at the point the machine is ended. Cricut maintains whatever authority is needed to suspend support for certain renditions of their product whenever, which can make a few cartridges quickly out of date.

The Cricut Craft Room programming empowers clients to join pictures from different cartridges, consolidate pictures, and stretch/turn pictures; it doesn't take into account the formation of discretionary designs. It additionally empowers the client to see the pictures showed on-screen before starting the cutting procedure, so the final product can be seen in advance.

Refering to Adobe's surrender of Flash, Cricut declared it would close Cricut Craft Room on 15 July 2018. Clients of "heritage" machines were offered a markdown to refresh to models good with Cricut Design Space. Starting at 16 July 2018, Design Space is the main programming accessible to make projects. Design Space isn't perfect with cartridges once in the past bought for the Cricut Mini, which was power nightfall in October 2018.

Third-party

Provo Craft has been effectively unfriendly to the utilization of outsider programming programs that could empower Cricut proprietors to remove designs and to utilize the machine without relying upon its exclusive cartridges. In a similar audit of bite the dust cutting machines, survey site TopTenReviews identified being "restricted to cutting designs from a gathering of cartridges" as a noteworthy downside of the Cricut run;

34

however, the audit noticed that it could be an inclination for some.

Two projects which could once in the past be utilized to make and after that get Cricut machines to remove subjective designs (utilizing, for instance, self-assertive TrueType text styles or SVG group illustrations) were Make-the-Cut (MTC) and Craft Edge's Sure Cuts A Lot (SCAL). In April 2010 Provo Craft opened lawful activity against the distributers of Make-the-Cut, and in January 2011 it sued Craft Edge to stop the conveyance of the SCAL program. In the two cases, the distributers settled with Provo Craft and expelled support for Cricut from their items. The projects keep on being usable with other home cutters.

As indicated by the content of its lawful grumbling against Craft Edge, "Provo Craft utilizes different strategies to encode and cloud the USB correspondences between Cricut DesignStudio [a design program provided with the hardware] and the Cricut e-shaper, so as to secure Provo Craft's restrictive programming and firmware, and to avoid endeavors to capture the cutting commands". Provo Craft battled that so as to comprehend and imitate this darkened convention, Craft Edge had dismantled the DesignStudio program, in opposition to the provisions of its End User License Agreement, along these lines (the organization affirmed) breaking copyright law. Provo Craft additionally affirmed that Craft Edge were damaging its trademark in "Cricut" by saying that its product could work with Cricut machines. Provo Craft declared this was likely "to cause perplexity, misstep or double dealing with regards to the source or starting point of Defendant's merchandise or benefits, and [was] prone to erroneously recommend a sponsorship, association, permit, or relationship of Defendant's products and ventures with Provo Craft."

The consequence of this is clients with more seasoned variants of Cricut machines that were 'power dusk' by stopping of programming bolster have no elective programming to use with their now outdated machines.

HOW TO START USING THE CRICUT MACHINE EVEN WITH NO EXPERIENCE

If you have been pondering about how to utilize Cricut Design Space with your Cricut, then this post is for you! This post will clarify the nuts and bolts of the program alongside certain tips which will enable you to make amazing designs with your Cricut machine

To begin with, how about we open up Cricut Design Space. You will see a screen like the one underneath. You can choose the "New Project" catch, or you can likewise peruse any of the Ready to Make extends in the "Included Projects" area. Prepared to Make ventures are ventures that are as of now accomplished for you and are overly amazing!

You will see beside my "New Project" catch I have my more established tasks that I have spared. If I needed to make or alter one of them, I can likewise choose one of them.

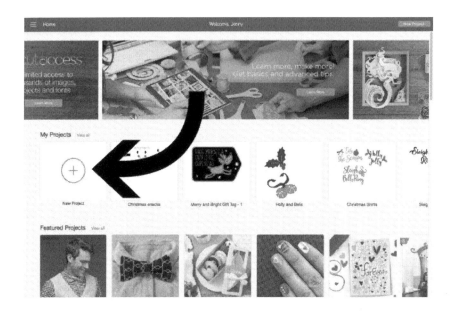

The most effective method to Use a Cricut: Setup

Cricut Explore Air 2 Machine

First of all, how about we investigate the machine itself and work out what each element does.

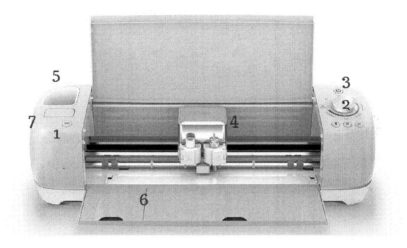

Catch to open cover

Brilliant Set Dial

Power on/off

Double cartridge (this is the place the sharp edges and pens are housed when you're utilizing them)

Adornment cup

Two adornment drawers

Cartridge port (into which you can plug any Cricut cartridges)

Making Space for the Cricut

Presently you've unloaded your fresh out of the box new Cricut machine, and you'll have to set it up, so it's prepared to begin cutting.

Regardless of whether you have a devoted specialty room or you're just making on your lounge area table, all you need is a level surface and access to control — recollect you can generally utilize an expansion lead if you're attempting to draw near enough to an attachment!

Ensure that there's some free space around the Cricut so you can load tangles all through the machine effectively.

When it's set up, you can connect the machine to an electrical plug (there's a power link included with each buy) and press the 'open' catch on the cover of the Cricut (highlight #1 in the delineation above) to open up the spic and span machine.

Adjacent, you have to set up the PC that you'll be designing on.

This could be a full work station, a PC, tablet, or even your telephone. Ensure that you approach the web so you can download and begin utilizing the Cricut Design Space application (more on that later).

An incredible aspect concerning the Cricut Explore Air 2 is the way that it's remote thus doesn't expect you to connection up your PC and the machine so as to begin designing.

When you've signed into the Design Space application, you'll have the option to interface your PC and the Cricut together remotely.

Step by step instructions to Use Design Space

Incorporated into the bundle with your fresh out of the box new art cutting machine will be a bit of paper guiding you to download Cricut Design Space.

This connection will walk you, well ordered, through the set-up procedure and will even tell you the best way to connect and control on your machine on the off chance that you haven't done that as of now.

Right off the bat, you'll have to ensure that Bluetooth is empowered on your PC, tablet or telephone.

Contingent upon the kind of model you're utilizing, you can, for the most part, discover the Bluetooth highlight under 'Settings' — simply ensure that it's on.

If you haven't as of now, turn on your Cricut by quickly holding down the power catch on the correct hand side of the machine

With your telephone or PC's Bluetooth settings open, pay special mind to CricutAIR spring up in the gadgets list. When you see it, click on it and associate.

You might be incited to enter a password now: utilize 0000 if so.

If, for reasons unknown, you can't get the Bluetooth to work or you basically don't have it on your gadget, just interface your PC and the Cricut utilizing the included USB link.

When you're set, your PC and Cricut will be connected together and prepared to go.

All that is left to do presently is begin designing!

What's extraordinary about Design Space is that it's uncommonly designed for fledglings thus gives well ordered direction on the most proficient method to begin and complete each venture. It's so natural to utilize that progressively experienced clients really discover it somewhat prohibitive — yet there's no compelling reason to stress over that until some other time!

Utilizing the Design Space App

We would prescribe downloading the Design Space application, which is as of now accessible completely on iOS and in a beta adaptation for Android frameworks.

The application is cloud-based, which implies that you'll have the option to get to your designs and record on any gadget that has the application. It's optimal for individuals who travel or for the individuals who need access to their Cricut record notwithstanding when they don't have web get to.

So as to design disconnected, just ensure that you download any pictures and textual styles you need to utilize in advance. To spare activities for disconnected use, tap the spare symbol and select 'spare as,' then spare to your gadget (instead of the cloud).

When you need to get to your tasks while you're disconnected, just draw down the classifications menu and select 'My Projects on this iPad' (or whatever gadget you're utilizing) and open it from that point.

When you're in online mode, you'll see the essentially many different activities accessible in the application for you to appreciate, just as the chance to make designs completely sans preparation utilizing the 'new canvas' component.

Your First Cut

Most first-time Cricut clients will begin their cutting vocation by finishing the 'Appreciate Card' Project that comes included with the machine on buy.

This is an incredible method to slide yourself into the universe of art slicing and open you to the different parts of utilizing the Cricut Machine.

After you've connected up your PC and the Cricut, Design Space will provoke you to begin this task.

You should simply adhere to the well ordered directions that spring up onscreen, and utilize the apparatuses and extras that were given in the bundle.

Simple peasy!

When you've finished your first cut, you'll likely be feeling somewhat more certain to take on progressively intriguing and difficult undertakings.

CRICUT MAKER—OVERALL REDESIGN

The principal enormous improvement for the Cricut Maker is that it has up to 10x the cutting weight of the Cricut Explore—4kg. This is in excess of a great deal of business cutting machines! I'm not catching that's meaning for the normal buyer? You would now be able to cut thicker and denser materials all the more effectively, including calfskin, chipboard, and wood up to 3/32″ thick. It can likewise cut the most sensitive of materials, similar to crepe paper. Additionally, it can cut texture! All o fthis, and it proceeds to beautifully cut the majority of the paper, vinyl, and different materials your Cricut Explore has constantly cut. Here are my posts about cutting Maker-just materials:

Basswood

Chipboard

Matboard

Calfskin (coming 4/3/19)

Texture

The subsequent improvement is the Adaptive Tool System. The Cricut Maker has considerably more power over the apparatuses, utilizing progressed scientific calculations and an arrangement of complex metal riggings designed to improve cutting exactness. The Adaptive Tool System permits Cricut to design new devices that can be included as they are concocted. For example, the Knife Blade and the Scoring Wheel are two new apparatuses that have been included since the dispatch, notwithstanding the Rotary Blade that accompanies the Maker.

Some littler upgrades incorporate a docking station for your telephone or iPad while dealing with your tasks just as a USB plug for charging those gadgets (I'm speculating this USB port will likewise power apparatuses eventually—only a hypothesis!). Apparatus stockpiling has been improved with two device cups and a bigger stockpiling receptacle.

It's likewise darn provocative, with a champagne gold top and precious stone carving all through. It feels like an Apple item, with design and client involvement with the highest priority on the rundown of Cricut's needs.

CRICUT MAKER ROTARY BLADE + SEWING FEATURES

My supreme most loved component of the Cricut Maker is the Rotary Blade, which accompanies the machine! The Cricut Explore can cut reinforced (texture with a stabilizer joined); however, it wasn't one of its solid suits—the fine point sharp edge is simply not reason designed for cutting texture. Look at my post on cutting texture here.

The Cricut Maker, then again, was designed in light of texture. Cricut needed to address one of the most tedious and frequently loathed pieces of sewing designs—cutting and denoting your texture. This is a major one for me. I have tendonitis in my grasp and utilizing scissors, or even a standard turning shaper can leave me with throbbing hands for a considerable length of time. It's one reason I haven't sewn a ton over the most recent couple of years.

Fortunately, Cricut made the inconceivable 12mm rotating sharp edge, designed specifically to cut straight texture—no support or stabilizer required! They have likewise made another pink texture tangle, with a totally different glue.

Viewing the Cricut Maker cut texture is inconceivable. So many-sided, so exact, no drag—and after that to strip the texture off the tangle with no quarrel is a wonderful thing!

Also, they have a launderable texture pen, which will—sewing aficionados, are you tuning in?— mark your textures for you. I loathe checking designs, so this is an enormous arrangement for me!

They have very couple of computerized sewing designs in the Design Space library and have banded together with brands like Simplicity and Riley Blake to include much more. The vast majority of the tasks are on the littler side since the Cricut Maker is still only a 12″ x 24″ max. In any case, it additionally encourages you make bigger activities that have littler pieces, similar to quilts! Pick a task, and the machine cuts every one of the pieces you need and checks them in like manner. (You can likewise mood killer the stamping highlight if you like to fly on a whim.) Some undertakings will be incorporated into Cricut Access, and some will be somewhere in the range of $2.99 and $9.99 for an example.

CRICUT MAKER KNIFE BLADE

To empower cutting those thicker materials, Cricut designed the Knife Blade. Utilized like you would utilize a x-acto knife, the knife sharp edge is brilliantly designed to cut utilizing a few passes—a lighter scoring line, then more power slicing through the center of the material, and consummation with a lighter go to get a well put together.

CORING WHEEL

In 2018, Cricut discharged the Scoring Wheel, as an update to the Scoring Stylus. As a papercrafter, I truly love the scoring wheel—it fixes the majority of your scoring misfortunes! If you're burnt out on black out score lines or breaking materials, the Cricut Scoring Wheel is an unquestionably improvement.

When the Cricut Maker was reported last August, I was truly eager to find out about the Adaptive Tool System. Fundamentally, the Adaptive Tool System implies that the carriage (the piece of the Cricut that holds the instruments) offers 10x the weight abilities as the Explore and isn't constrained to the devices initially designed for the machine. Rather, it enabled Cricut to grow new instruments and applications. We've seen the Rotary Blade and the Knife Blade, and now we have the Scoring Wheel.

WHICH CRICUT USES THE SCORING WHEEL?

Both Cricut Scoring Wheels are a piece of the Adaptive Tool System on the Cricut Maker, so they must be utilized with the Cricut Maker. These scoring wheels won't work with the Explore or more established machines.

WOULDN'T I BE ABLE TO JUST USE MY SCORING STYLUS?

Indeed! You can even now utilize your Scoring Stylus on any collapsing undertakings. In any case, if you've found in the past that your Scoring Stylus hasn't given you the outcomes you'd like, the Scoring Wheel will tackle those issues. Peruse along to find out about how the Scoring Stylus differs from the Scoring Wheels.

WHAT PROBLEMS DOES THE SCORING WHEEL SOLVE?

Perhaps the greatest protest with the Scoring Stylus was that it didn't make profound enough score lines. There were ways around this (multiplying the score line in Cricut Design Space, for instance); however, swoon score lines were unquestionably a dissatisfaction for certain crafters. The Scoring Wheels, then again, make a decent, even, unmistakable score line on basically every material utilizing something like 10x more weight than the Scoring Stylus.

Another issue that the scoring wheel understands is breaking when you overlay your materials. If you've utilized thicker or covered papers or card stock previously, you'll realize that nothing will destroy a collapsed undertaking quicker than split materials. Fortunately, the twofold scoring wheel makes broke material a relic of days gone by! How about we figure out how.

WHY TWO SCORING WHEELS?

The Scoring Wheel is really two instruments in one. There is one principle lodging and two different scoring wheels that you can change out as required. To change, simply push the plunger on the highest point of the lodging to evacuate one haggle on the other wheel.

THE SINGLE SCORING WHEEL

The single Scoring Wheel is the immediate advance up from the Scoring Stylus. It scores precisely like the Scoring Stylus does; however, your lines will be more profound and more even than with the Scoring Stylus.

THE DOUBLE SCORING WHEEL

Like I referenced above, if you've at any point utilized covered materials with the Cricut Scoring Stylus, you'll realize that these thicker claim to fame materials tend to break. Cricut's splendid specialists have concocted a rich answer for assistance with this issue—the Double Scoring Wheel.

Fundamentally, the Double Scoring Wheel makes two parallel score lines directly beside one another. The twofold score takes into account within the crease to "breakdown" neatly—it truly is the ideal answer for those covered and thicker materials.

HOW MIGHT I TELL MY SCORING WHEELS APART?

The single scoring wheel has "01" engraved on it, and the twofold scoring wheel has "02" engraved on it. Looking carefully, you can differentiate also, yet utilizing the numbers is the least demanding approach to distinguish the two wheels.

WHAT MATERIALS CAN I SCORE WITH MY CRICUT SCORING WHEEL?

I have made a helpful dandy graph for you! These are only an example of the considerable number of materials that can be scored, and which Scoring Wheels are prescribed. There are more—play around with your specific material!

ALL THINGS CONSIDERED USING THE SCORING WHEEL

Here are a couple of things to remember when utilizing the Scoring Wheel on your activities.

The scoring wheel shouldn't be adjusted like the Knife Blade.

If no doubt about it paper (like sparkle card stock), reflect your task and put the truly side of your paper face down on your tangle. The score lines will then be in the back and will crease appropriately.

When you go to make your undertaking, Cricut Design Space will disclose to you which Scoring Wheel to utilize, in view of the material you've chosen.

In contrast to utilizing the Scoring Stylus, you really need to swap out the Scoring Wheel with the cutting edge you're going to utilize. Your undertaking will score first, and then you'll be coordinated to expel the Wheel and addition your sharp edge to cut.

I've utilized mine on a couple of undertakings up until now and I am overwhelmed by how much better it is from the Scoring Stylus. What's more, that is in the wake of reasoning that the Stylus is in reality quite incredible! In any case, the Scoring Wheel's lines are so smooth and even and now my undertakings overlay so effectively. You can make this equivalent little box venture in Cricut's Ready To Make area in Cricut Design Space!

WHERE CAN I BUY THE CRICUT SCORING WHEEL?

At the present time, the Scoring Wheel is just accessible in Cricut's online store. Request has been high, so frequently it's sold out. Yet, continue returning—they are getting new shipments constantly.

PRINT THEN CUT IMPROVEMENTS

I've been utilizing the Print Then Cut element increasingly more for brisk activities on my Cricut Explore. The greatest confinement to the Explore, notwithstanding, was that the sensor could just peruse enlistment checks on white paper. The new sensor in the Cricut Maker has been reengineered and would now be able to be utilized with hued paper (not by any stretch of the imagination dull paper—yet who prints on extremely dim paper at any rate?). If that wasn't already enough, it additionally chips away at many printed papers—it wasn't generally what Cricut proposed; however, it's an incredible reward! They've additionally adjusted the enlistment stamps inside Design Space with the goal that you can utilize a greater amount of the printable region on a sheet of paper (this is for all machines, not simply the Cricut Maker).

DO I NEED A CRICUT MAKER?

So the unavoidable issue is—do you truly need to update? There were some disillusioned individuals via web-based networking media who had quite recently obtained an Explore and were miserable to discover this new machine was simply propelled (trust me, I get it—I truly purchased a business warmth press two weeks before the Cricut EasyPress was reported!).

The beneficial thing is the line of Cricut Explore machines isn't leaving. There is as yet bolster accessible for these machines, and they will, in any case, turn out with new undertakings and designs that can be cut on the Explore. For my perusers specifically, the greater part of my future ventures and slice records will almost certainly be cut on the Explore just as the Maker. Be that as it may, I am eager to handle a portion of these new materials, as well!

So how about we get down to essentials: if you couldn't care less about cutting texture or thicker materials, your Cricut Explore will keep on serving you truly well—I've had one for a long time and still arrangement on utilizing mine! If you are truly keen on cutting texture and sewing ventures, or if you need to attempt it for carpentry or calfskin working, you may consider updating. Regardless of what decision you make, you'll have an extraordinary machine designed by a creative organization!

DESIGN SPACE SOFTWARE SECRETS

Configuration spaces programming is a workmanship. It's the result of soul, not the product of deductive examiners. There isn't a calculation, strategy, example, procedure, or fake plot that can make great programming.

Programming is an inventive work of art driven by a dream. The dream is taken advantage of by concentrated ingenuity, center, thought, and long periods of readiness. It prompts snapshots of understanding, trailed by a long stretch of time of reasoning, coding, and thinking some more. This is the place incredible structure originates from.

Profound Knowledge

Be that as it may, don't misunderstand me, I don't lounge around and trust that my dream will come. Dreams work like a fantastic feast—with great fixings.

The crude materials of configuration may be documentation, a perfect workbench, studio, easels, paints, ability, and information. A performer has to know scales. A painter needs to get tones. A stone carver needs a sharp eye for negative space. An essayist must have a feeling of style.

For the most elevated fixings, a craftsman needs to examine every one of the works that preceded, both great and awful. A decent Design spaces softwareer ponders how things work in their field.

This is, so the fashioner isn't tottered by obliviousness or dirtied by assumptions. Wide introduction to the art places things conversely more plainly.

Hard Practice

Learning alone, however, doesn't convert into aptitude. We expand on the establishment with a long stretch of time of training.

It doesn't make a difference if the training occurs at the easel, composing work area, or workbench. Creatives since forever have drawn from artistic creations of the experts, and composed awful tune after terrible tune until they got to the great ones.

Creators practice to the point that the art turns out to be natural. It resembles contact composing on the console. At the point when the dream strikes, we make without the slightest hesitation.

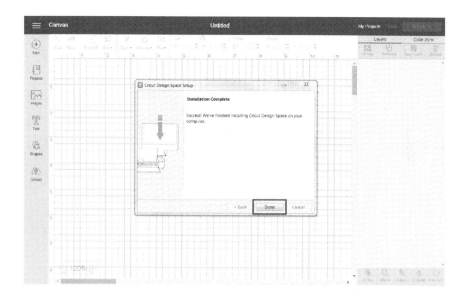

A decent artist can tune in to a tune and figure out its structure. A decent coder can see a UI and in a split second picture the fundamental code's structure. Some of the time, the psychological picture is superior to the first.

A decent coder can take a gander at code they haven't seen previously and begin discussing how it functions. Watchwords rise up out of letters. Thoughts spring from images and blank area. Dreams of registers and arrangements show up alongside mental illustrations of boxes, lines, and bolts.

Code is the plan similarly composing is. When the words are on paper, the author shouldn't be engaged with the production forms. There are a lot of individuals who can print books and convey them to stores. The craftsmanship is in the words.

For the coder, the "distributing staff" is the compiler and loader. This product transforms plan into something of administration.

The principal program I, at any point composed, as straightforward as it might have been, showed me this. Coding was mysterious in that I could outline something on paper, lift it up, and go. Maybe I could draw a motor, and it would simply work. Or then again, not work; however I could redraw it. There was no long procedure of making each part and manufacturing them out of metal or collecting the sleek chaos before testing. I just incorporated my structure.

This high workmanship isn't generally so high. It's what ought not out of the ordinary of everybody who brings home the bacon programming for general society. It's a gifted calling that asks for motivation and makes progress toward increasingly elevated polished methodology.

Without a doubt, you can hack code together like you can rapidly complete a paint by numbers. It resembles these sites I see with heaps of short, without content posts spewing oxymoronic "tried and true way of thinking." They're frequently composed by individuals who read 500-word computerized showcasing presents about how on put similarly wobbly "content offers" behind email dividers. It resembles noting a paper promotion on the most proficient method to profit in the classifieds, burning through $9.99 just to discover it's to run advertisements about how to profit in the classifieds.

Without a doubt, you can utilize Grady-Booch's strategy and power a lot of developers into an inflexible and religious deft arrangement. They'll trudge on always and make increasingly more code that does less and less. The swell and bugs will develop into a moderate, deadened, self-serving mess all gratitude to a misinformed supervisory crew determined to make easy money either by IPO or securing by a bigger organization. Everybody will forsake the code for the following startup in a ceaseless semiannual walk to obscurity.

Certainly, you can do that. What's more, you can exact torment and enduring on the client, the destitute individual who is unconscious of security ruptures, structure techniques, light-footed associations, and enormous programming vaults dissipated more than several workstations.

All that those poor clients see are bugs and confounding interfaces that moderate with each discharge. Never in the historical backdrop of the world has so much staggering equipment done as such little for such huge numbers of.

Learning of the User

Configuration spaces programming, similar to all structure, must focus on the client. They are the explanation behind the product in any case. Something worth being thankful for about present day ways to deal with programming improvement, in any event in their unique pronouncements, is their acknowledgment of this reality.

They request that the client is included. They should be fused into the procedure, sharing thoughts regarding what works, what doesn't, and why.

In any case, some way or another this mission loses all sense of direction in the board's execution of these methodologies. They run along without a client in sight. It's to the point where spry organizations look somewhat like coordinated improvement. It's anything but difficult to perceive any reason why the client is lost when individuals work 18 hour days to include each half-working component the board requests.

Regardless of whether the Design spaces programming incorporates the client, it's insufficient in light of the fact that it's uncommon that a client comprehends information structures. Counseling clients is great, accepting they can enable the creator to consider the structure; however a software engineer must know the client's experience personally. Fashioners need to do the client's activity for some time and sympathize with the client's agony.

This procedure doesn't just most recent daily. It takes as long as it must for the software engineer to instinctually observe answers for the client's issues. I've realized fashioners to ride in an emergency vehicle every night for two or three months. The framework to help emergency vehicle drivers that they made was awesome. There is no swap for comprehension.

Calm

In the wake of structure information, rehearsing hard, and figuring out how to see the world through the client's eyes, it's a great opportunity to get tranquil. Stop. Think. Sketch. Pause. Hold up some more, and in the end, the thoughts will begin streaming.

Once in a while, it takes some time. Once in a while, the musings you had during the exploration part of the improvement spring to life rapidly, however typically not. When it begins, however, it floods. Keep a note pad, a heap of paper, or an application close by. Whatever you use, hold writing down the out of this world.

Language is a baffling thing. Verbalization makes contemplations. Musings make words which thusly improve contemplations. This is the procedure before plan. A story is constantly helpful.

Presently begin coding. Aggregate soon, and accumulate regularly. Think. Assemble. Test. On the off chance that you don't care for "test," call it "running," yet do the circle commonly 60 minutes. Coders are beguiling themselves with cases that they can envision every one of the odds and ends and afterward simply compose. You should code. Code is the plan!

Where to begin is as much a motivation as the general arrangement of assault. Rely upon the dream for that also. Regularly the spot to begin is the place the information enters the framework. Or on the other hand, it may be the piece of the framework that catches your eye most. Different occasions, it's ideal to assault the most overwhelming parts. Like mythical beasts, they should be transformed into windmills.

Anyway, you begin, code. Code like the breeze. Toss stuff out and code once more. Fred Brooks said you can't generally compose a prerequisite report on the grounds that such huge numbers of the necessities are implanted in the plan itself. You can't characterize the interfaces first; however you should end with great interfaces. The best way to do that is to make, toss bits out, and endeavor once more.

None of this is conceivable except if you get tranquil and let the breeze blow in thoughts. Tune in for the dream. On the off chance that it's moderate in coming, compose little odds and ends and pause. In the event that you pause, accepting you have the learning, practice, and love for your clients, the dream will come. It's as certain and characteristic as a supported seed growing.

When it at last comes, begin. Code will rise and develop in layers. Code will be hurled. Alter, order, test, rehash. You'll have splendid thoughts and not know where they originated from. It's everything from the dream. Who knows where the breeze blows?

Adaptability

A few people make all the more successfully on a fixed calendar. John Cheever went to a cellar office for eight hours consistently. Others of us need to make the most of current opportunities, regardless of great importance.

Tune in to your very own innovativeness, and realize what works best for you. Ken Thompson's hours pivot on a more prominent than 24-hour plan. Dennis Ritchie would appear for lunch, go through the evening at Murray Hill, return home, sit in front of the TV, and afterward work until the early morning. We, as a whole need to figure out how we work best.

Imagination and configuration are natural in each one of us. Simply perused all the more broadly and you'll see that I'm not saying anything new. Authors, painters, and arrangers have taken in this. Our cosmetics is simply youthful and getting more youthful constantly. The normal software engineer is still in their twenties. Youth, particularly those that attention on innovation, frequently neglect to investigate the best pieces of the humanities. Subsequently, there are rushes of software engineers that need to get familiar with these human parts of their calling, again and again, acknowledging why Donald Knuth titled his book The Art of Computer Programming.

For what reason do we neglect to hang tight for the dream? For what reason does it take a negligible seven years for the product world to relapse once again into supposing it can timetable plan?

I speculate it is a should be in charge. During a time of two-day shipping, we hope to make on interest. This need seeps into all parts of life. We are the moment society, and we should have everything quick. What's more, it.

GETTING STARTED IN THE NEW CRICUT DESIGN SPACE

First, you must remove the old program from your computer by accessing your control panel. Then you will go to Cricut and download the new software. Follow the on-screen instructions after downloading.

After downloading the new software, start exploring! There are changes, and some things are the same. Here are some of my observations:

NEW CRICUT DESIGN SPACE HOME SCREEN

First, the home screen is a little different and easy to navigate.

Choose a new project or click on one of your saved projects.

CRICUT DESIGN SPACE CANVAS OPTIONS

When you're on another task or Canvas, you have practically indistinguishable choices from far as embeddings pictures.

Pictures is for Cricut pictures and tasks.

Snap on TEXT to add content to your undertaking (more instructional exercises coming later on this).

Snap on SHAPES to embed different premade shape alternatives.

You can likewise UPLOAD your very own pictures.

When you embed any of these things, you can tap on the limit bolts to turn, resize, and open the measurements.

DESIGN SPACE TOOL BAR UPDATES

The LAYERS board has moved a few instruments from the upper right side to the base right side (Slice, Weld, Attach, Flatten, and Contour).

Gathering, Ungroup, copy, and erase are presently at the highest point of the layers board.

You can, in any case, pick layer qualities by tapping on the layer inside the board. Pick whether to cut, compose, score, or print. You can likewise pick hues and examples for print things.

Alter is no longer in the correct side board. Everything will currently be at the highest point of the page (fix, adjust, orchestrate, resize, and so forth)

The TEXT alter bar will likewise show up at the highest point of the page when you click on a thing with content.

You'll have the option to pick Cricut textual styles, or custom textual styles, the style, size, dispersing, arrangement, and propelled alternatives for content editing.

Transfer FILE UPDATES TO DESIGN SPACE

I'll be going into A LOT more detail with this, yet I figured you might want a little see to transferring documents to the new Cricut DS! The greatest change is that Printable records would now be able to be bigger. The greatest size is presently 8.75 in X 6.25 in. It used to be 8 in X 5 in. It may not appear to be a tremendous difference; however it makes my life SO a lot simpler with a portion of my printable undertakings! You can likewise relocate documents as opposed to looking through organizers for the correct one.

11 REASONS YOU NEED A CRICUT ACCESS SUBSCRIPTION

If you're wavering about getting that Cricut Access Subscription, this rundown may enable you to choose. There are such a large number of instant designs you can make with your Cricut Explore Air!

You realize I adore causing my own designs to use with my Cricut To investigate, yet here and there if I have to make a genuine snappy art, I realize I can discover something stunning with my Cricut Access Subscription. For Week Four of the 24 Week Cricut Series, I'm going over the numerous reasons you ought to consider pursuing Cricut Access!

Likewise note that Cricut Access is for use with the Cricut Explore just, so if you have a more seasoned model and this sounds like something you need, you might need to consider redesigning!

NO DESIGN EXPERIENCE NECESSARY WITH CRICUT ACCESS PROJECTS

I cherish working with Make it Now Projects because you truly simply press two or three catches. You perceive how to did that to make the beautiful support gift encloses you see the picture above. You can utilize any paper you like, and the Cricut basically does practically everything for you!

EFFECTIVELY CUSTOMIZE GRAPHICS IN CRICUT ACCESS

By and by, this requires close to nothing, if any design understanding, however you can customize any Make it Now extends or different illustrations in the Cricut Access library as I did with this Boho Feather Decor Project.

HUGE GRAPHIC LIBRARY

Cricut has more than 30,000 pictures that are incorporated into Cricut Access! They've additionally made scanning for pictures such a great amount of simpler, as should be obvious in my post, My FAVORITE Updates to Cricut Design Space. Odds are, if you need a specific realistic, Cricut Access will have one incorporated into your membership. It incorporates single cut pictures, 3D ventures, multi-layered pictures, and the sky is the limit from there! You get moment access to every one of these pictures once you sign up.

ENORMOUS FONT LIBRARY

Alongside designs and tasks, Cricut Acess additionally incorporates more than 370 text styles! I LOVE me a few textual styles, so this is a noteworthy in addition to for me. If you're just in it for the text styles, Cricut has a Fonts just Subscription!

MARKDOWN ON GRAPHICS AND FONTS

Cricut makes them astound text styles and designs that are incorporated into access, yet if you see something in the store that you completely love (trust me... you will), you will get half off of a significant number of the things in the shop with a Premium Subscription and 10% off with a Standard Subscription. Note: The half rebate does exclude things from some authorized organizations, so ensure you read what is incorporated.

LIMITS ON PHYSICAL CRICUT PRODUCTS

If the markdown on computerized items doesn't get you, then perhaps a 10% rebate on Physical items may influence you. If you are making numerous Cricut ventures a month, this membership you could save money on vinyl, mats, and other Cricut supplies.

SELECTIVE SALES FOR CRICUT ACCESS MEMBERS

Alongside the regular investment funds, you'll likewise get notified of elite advancements and deals. By and by, if you plan on making a great deal of undertakings with your Cricut consistently, this could truly prove to be useful.

Since we have a portion of the advantages of Cricut Access Membership, we should discuss every one of the things you can CREATE with Cricut Access.

SIMPLE PARTY DECOR CREATION

I think my companion Britni completed a breathtaking activity with her Summer First Birthday Party, and she made quite a bit of her stylistic theme with Cricut Access ventures! Try not to misunderstand me, arranging a gathering is a LOT of work, yet in any event with Cricut Access, you'll have a significant part of the design work accomplished for you. I very suggest looking through the immense gathering of illustrations and Make it Now extends before arranging your next gathering.

MAKE UNIQUE PROJECTS

Something I never truly figured I would make is adornments; however the Cricut made that conceivable. I had a ton of fun making my own design for a Faux Leather Bracelet, yet this Butterfly Necklacemade with a Cricut Access Project is AMAZING, right??? I simply love that you can get innovative with effectively made ventures. I'm additionally cherishing this Wet Bathing Suit Bag... virtuoso, isn't that so?

EFFECTIVELY CREATE HOMEMADE GIFTS

You could actually make all that you requirement for the ideal gift with designs from Cricut Access. From the Homemade Gift Card to a fun gift like these DIY Dish Towels, Cricut has you secured!

MAKE GORGEOUS HOME DECOR

I utilize my Cricut all the ideal opportunity for home stylistic layout. I cherish my Gigantic Floral Vinyl Walls that I made with my own design; however you can without much of a stretch do likewise with a Cricut Access Project. Another fun adornment thought is this Felt Board with a 3D Flower!

Thus, primary concern... if you utilize your Cricut Explore regularly and need to make extends quicker, Cricut Access is unquestionably for you!

SUREFIRE WAYS TO MAKE MONEY WITH YOUR CRICUT

1. SET OUT TO BE DIFFERENT

Extremely simply act naturally. Carry your idiosyncrasy and imagination to the table.

If you've been around Cricut makes for any time allotment I'm certain you're acquainted with the knockout name tiles. They are an insane hit and soon everybody was selling them.

That is how it goes in the creating scene, isn't that right? So you could be one of the primary individuals to bounce on a pattern ride the wave until the following hot vender goes along. Be that as it may, that technique for selling Cricut specialties can end up tedious and expensive if you're not cautious.

Remember I'm not guiding you to re-imagine the wheel here, however to include your very own style and energy.

Investigate the image underneath. It's of two name tiles I found on Etsy. The one on the top column looks simply like the other 150 available to be purchased on Etsy.

The merchant on the base included her own turn things. Which one stands apart more? Which dealer can charge more and make a higher benefit?

Try not to be reluctant to change text styles either. You can discover super arrangements and complimentary gifts for premium textual styles at fontbundles.net Something that basic will make you stand apart from the horde of 'I Love Glitter' textual styles.

Because the thing is when your specialty looks like everybody else's, then it just turns into a value war. No one successes.

So when every other person zigs, you zoom. OK?

2. KEEP IT NARROW

I was one of the occasion organizers for a show this Summer. One of my co-organizers declared that she had a shirt young lady and was having custom shirts made for us.

Ummm helllo? They all realize I have a Cricut. I can make shirts. I would simply charge cost - if that.

Yet, her brain went directly to her shirt young lady. Why? Because the shirt young lady just does shirts and she does them well.

I do painted signs and decals coincidentally. So when somebody needs one of those they consider me. I know another person who simply does hoops. Also, we've even got somebody who just papers blooms.

You may think making and selling all things everywhere will give you more assortment, hence more clients, along these lines more cash. Be that as it may, that is not the manner in which it works.

What it will give you is more cost, more burnout, and more items not selling.

Try not to intend to be the Walmart of the specialty world, expect to be a specialist and the best there is in your general vicinity of slyness. So pause for a moment and choose what you will end up known for.

3. BE CONSISTENT

Work on your Cricut make business reliably. In a perfect world, you ought to chip away at it consistently. Some of you may simply need to sell as a pastime and can just take a shot at it once every week.

Whatever your timetable is do it as reliably as possible. You're never going to go anyplace if you overlook your business for a considerable length of time or months one after another.

Be reliable with valuing and quality as well. Your clients should realize what's in store from you. They will prescribe you to others again and again if they realize they can rely on you.

4. PERSISTENT WINS

See, I don't wanna be Debbie Downer here, however owning a business can in some cases suck.

What's more, if you need to transform this thing into a business, there will be days you need to stop.

There will be days clients will tick you off. There will be days that nothing works right. You're busting your butt and getting no place quick.

Stop. Take a full breath. Like I said it is anything but a pyramid scheme. The individuals that didn't discover achievement, they quit sometime in the past. In any case, you... .. you my companion draw up your young lady undies and continue onward.

Because the individuals who succeed never surrender. They may have disappointments. In any case, that doesn't stop them. Never. Give. Up.

5. YOU WANT HOW MUCH?

I genuinely can't accept how often this occurs... ... Someone buys decals from me so she can make and sell sparkle tumblers. That is not the mind boggling part...

I calmly approached her the amount she charged for a tumbler because well my better half detests sparkle lol. Be that as it may, the tumblers make magnificent gifts. Anyway, she disclosed to me her cost and I shouted wow that is too modest.

Furthermore, she reacted yea I HOPE I'M NOT LOSING MONEY

I'm sorry WHAT? You HOPE you aren't losing cash? Goodness nectar.

You need to know the expense. If you're selling something for $20 and it costs you $22 in provisions, that is bad! Not great by any means.

I know there are a few things like sparkle and epoxy for this situation that might be difficult to figure. You don't have the foggiest idea what number of tumblers one container of sparkle will cover until you arrive at the finish of your sparkle container. (follow along, coincidentally, take a marker and put a hash mark on the sparkle container for each tumbler you make)

Be that as it may, you can guestimate. If it would appear that you utilized around 1/4 of the container and the container costs $10, take 10 and gap it by 4 and you have a sparkle cost of $2.50 per tumbler per shade of sparkle. So two shades of sparkle is a $5.00 sparkle cost. Tailing me?

For the love of everything sly please experience the majority of your provisions and include the expenses. After I have all the huge things included up I for the most part include a $1.00 or two for the cost supplies that I use, yet utilize such a little amount it's not worth figuring up. Paste is a case of that.

When you have the expense of provisions you'll be better arranged to value your things to sell. Remember the time it took you to make the thing except if you like working for nothing.

A general standard guideline is your selling cost will be between two to multiple times your expense of provisions. Try not to stress over individuals snickering at you that it's excessively. You're unique, you've limited your field and you're a specialist and the best at what you do. Additionally you're utilizing quality items (more on that soon).

Individuals WILL happily pay for that.

6. GAIN SOME NEW USEFUL KNOWLEDGE EVERYDAY

Try not to fear gaining from the individuals who have gone before you. You don't need to figure everything out individually.

Regardless of whether you need to figure out how to climb the Etsy positions or assemble a fruitful facebook gathering, somebody has just done it and now they are showing every one of the tips and deceives they know.

At any rate toward the beginning of your Cricut business, you'll be accomplishing more promoting than creating. Make it an objective to gain some new useful knowledge consistently that relates to your business.

7. QUALITY CONTROL

Sell quality items. Quality successes over amount each day of the week.

So the two basins on the privilege are from the Dollar Tree. Everybody and their sibling sold these at Easter which kept the benefits low.

We realize the can cost is $1.00 and we will appraise the vinyl and move paper was $1.00 which gives us an expense of $2.00. I saw them available to be purchased for $5.00 every which means we make a benefit of $3.00 per container. They rush to make so not to terrible.

Easter goes back and forth, the pails presumably get overlooked or destroyed because they were economically made and modest to purchase.

Presently the Easter Baskets on the left. They are texture and clearly better quality. They stand apart because very few if some other crafters are selling them. You are adapting each day and you realize that if we simply put the name on them, these bins can be utilized well past Easter and we advertise them accordingly.

We paid $8.00 for the clear bin and $1.00 for the warmth move vinyl for a complete expense of $9.00. We are selling them for $25.00 which gives us a benefit of $16.00 for every one we sell.

Which means we can sell less and get more cash-flow. The crafter selling Dollar Store containers needs to make and sell 6 bins for each one we offer to make a similar benefit.

Give that sink access a second. Less work implies more opportunity for family or fun or learning.

Individuals will pay for quality and they will prescribe you to their companions for quality. Verbal promoting is as well as can be expected get.

Pick quality items.

Where to Buy Quality Blanks for Cricut Crafts

I have two places that I like to purchase quality spaces for making that I'll impart to you.

The first is called My Vinyl Direct and it's found here. They have an incredible determination and all that I have requested from them has been extraordinary.

HOW TO REALIZE AND EDIT CRICUT PROJECT IDEAS

When your machine has been enlisted, you will be prepared to make your first venture! Snap on the in addition to sign, "New Project." You will then observe a clear matrix example, and this space is called your "Canvas." This space is the place you make ANY of your materials and is your clear canvas.

From here, you will see to one side of your canvas screen, and you will see different symbols for different activities: Templates, Projects, Images, Text, Shapes, and Uploads. This is your vital aspect for making and causing anything you to can envision.

* The highest point of your screen will stay in the dim, incapable to tap on, state until you select your canvas by tapping on one of the symbols to one side of the screen.*

Layouts help you appropriately design a wide assortment of activities. From challises to T-shirts, you can tap the sort of item that you will put your completed design on, and it will give a visual picture of one for better position.

Activities incorporate a great many Ready to Make extends that will make them specialty immediately. You can likewise redo the majority of these if you like.

Pictures will carry you to a hunt screen where you can glance through a large number of pictures for your tasks.

Content will raise a case where you can type and alter any content that you wish to include.

Shapes is a simple method to include some fundamental shapes or a score line to your task.

Transfers enables you to get your very own pictures. The kinds of records that you can utilize are .jpg, .bmp, .png, .gif, .svg, and .dxf. Pursue the prompts on the screen to prepare it for use.

All Cricut Explore machines, just as the Maker, utilize the fine and profound cut edges. The Maker is the just one to utilize the Rotary edge.

To stack your cutting edge lodging, essentially open up the hook on your machine that has the "B" set apart on it. Take your cutting edge and drop it into spot and secure with the conclusion tab. You can change out the standard and profound cut cutting edges in their lodgings by evacuating it, pushing the catch on top, removing the top from the new sharp edge, and embeddings it into the lodging.

With the most up to date form of Cricut Design Space, altering content in the program couldn't be simpler! The content editing alternatives enable clients to make the ideal content for their uncommon task. There are a few choices that spring up in the word processing board and realizing what every one does enables clients to benefit as much as possible from their content editing. We should investigate all the word processing board decisions and how to alter message in Cricut Design Space.

To alter content, first, you should make the content. Start by opening up Cricut Design Space and after that "Another Project." Click the "T" on the left hand board. A clear box will show up. Type your content into the container. Cricut Design Space will populate the content in a default text style. Presently, it's an ideal opportunity to alter it!

Changing the Font Type

Snap the "Text style" alternative to change the textual style type. The text styles are separated into "Framework" textual styles and "Cricut Fonts." Cricut Fonts are ones that are accessible through Cricut Design Space. Some are accessible for nothing, others are accessible with a Cricut Access Subscription, and others require an extra charge. Framework Fonts are those that Cricut Design Space pulls from your PC. These incorporate textual styles that you may download from another source (my preferred text style hotspot for downloading text styles is Hungry JPEG). You may likewise channel text styles to incorporate those with a composition style (for a hand-lettered look) or single layer textual styles or multi-layer text styles. When you have discovered a textual style that you like, click on it to see the content in that specific textual style. If you are content with the decision, progress forward. If not, keep looking until you've discovered the ideal text style. Finding the best text style for my undertaking more often than not takes me some time!

The Font Style alternative enables clients to utilize their favored text style in customary, intense, italics, or composing style. In any case, not these choices will show up for each textual style. The style decisions will be different, as indicated by what is accessible for that text style.

Utilize the Font Size choice to make the content bigger or littler. If you don't have a clue about the definite number to resize the textual style, remember that you can generally make the content bigger or littler utilizing the bolt on the base right of the content box, as well.

Changing the Space between Letters

Did you realize that you can change the space between letters in Cricut Design Space? This is a marvelous element that keeps clients from composing and space each letter separately. Utilize the Letter Space choice to make the space between every individual letter bigger or littler.

Changing the Space between lines of content

This choice works when there is more than one line of content in the content box, as appeared in the photograph above. Use

Line Space increment or decline the space between the lines of content. This works for lines inside a similar content box.

Changing the Text Alignment

With the Text Alignment choice, clients can adjust content to one side, right, or focal point of the content box. Remember this does not adjust message inside the whole task itself, just inside the content box.

Propelled Text Tools

The Advanced catch takes into consideration ungrouping the content. The "Ungroup to Letters" enables client to ungroup the content to individual letters. The "Ungroup to Lines" enables the client to ungroup the content to individual lines. This alternative possibly works if there is more than one line of content in the content box. If you are utilizing a multi-layer text style, then you may likewise have an "Ungroup to Layers" choice accessible. When lines or letters have been ungrouped, clients can alter and control those letters or lines autonomously. I utilize the Advanced choice commonly to ungroup lines of content. Intermittently, I will have designed something in a content box and after that conclude that I wish to move the reality of content some place differently. The "Ungroup to Lines" proves to be useful for this. I utilize the "Ungroup to Letters" when bending content.

Bend Text

The Curve Text Icon is a hotly anticipated expansion to the content editing board in Cricut Design Space. I've made a post and video to show how to utilize this amazing new element. Peruse increasingly about it in Curving Text in Cricut Design Space.

How about we bend some content

Here we are going to include our stunning impact!

Select the primary line of content and snap on bend, and type -5.104, this will make the line to bend down.

Then, we will choose the second line of content, yet this time, we are going to type 5.104. This will make the line bend up.

At long last, for the third line of content, we are going to rehash something very similar we did with the principal line. Snap on bend and type - 5.104

Sort out the majority of the components

We should play with Linetype and Fill

Typically you would adhere to one Linetype; however, with the end goal of this instructional exercise, we are going to utilize the draw and cut and print alternatives.

For the principal line, I chose draw as a linetype, and after that, for shading, I went with a light turquoise.

For the subsequent line, I went with Cut as linetype to enact the fill choice. Then I chose print as fill and a turquoise shading.

For the last line, I needed to investigate designs! So I chose slice as linetype to initiate the fill alternative, and afterward, I changed the print type, for example.

There are numerous choices you can choose from; however, I needed to stay with the a turquoise design.

Things To Know Before Your First Cricut Maker Project

1. Your kitchen association is going to get Pinterest-commendable.

You realize every one of those adorable container names you've been sticking since 2013? You can make those now. Furthermore, you can tweak them anyway you need. However, spoiler alert, when your lady friends see what you've finished with your kitchen, you better accept they'll be requesting that you come over and name theirs as well. Let the Cricut Parties start!

Some incredible learner ventures for kitchen association are printing names for clear wash room holders, fridge cabinet names, and these Spice Jar names I made. A peruser contacted me on Instagram to demonstrate to me her prosperity from my instructional exercise, and it was her absolute first Cricut venture ever. What's more, let me tell ya, young lady, she ROCKED it!

2. You'll require a committed art space.

The Maker is a thick bit of hardware, and you'll require a decent workspace to utilize it. This is the ideal opportunity to cut out a space in your visitor room or the arbitrary niche in your lounge area that you never realized how to manage.

Regardless of whether it's only a little storage room like mine, it's very worth keeping all your art stuff in one available spot.

Prepared to begin setting up your art space? Here's your rundown of unquestionable requirements:

A work area, table, or ledge and a comfortable seat. Extra focuses if the seat has wheels.

Producer extra room. This machine isn't too overwhelming, yet it's not light either, so don't anticipate putting away it on a truly elevated or low rack. My preferred method to store it is on this moving truck; however, you can keep it anyplace that is anything but difficult to get to with insignificant exertion.

Great lighting. This is so significant because once you complete your video instructional exercises and get familiar with about weeding, you'll understand that you need your best pair of glasses and excessively splendid lights. That overhead light on your roof fan won't cut it. Go for LED undertaking lighting on your workspace.

Capacity holders. You may have begun by getting a group, or possibly you are simply purchasing supplies on a venture by-venture premise. Whatever course you take, you're going to wind up with a ton of things to store. Settle on clear lidded compartments to isolate your devices and supplies, and make sure to utilize that new Maker of yours to mark your holders, so everything remains decent and slick.

3. You'll need *ALL* the adornments.

Notwithstanding the Maker, Cricut has a ton of sweet frill that will make your tasks much smoother, quicker, simpler, and progressively expert looking.

My outright most loved extra instrument is the BrightPad. It's essentially similar to a tablet-molded light box that specialists use for following, and it makes weeding SO a lot simpler when you're doing multifaceted cuts.

I likewise exceptionally recommend snatching the Essential Kit, the Portable Trimmer, and the Extra Large Self-Healing Cutting Mat. I utilize these awful young men for each and every undertaking I do. Take it from the young lady who can't slice a straight line to spare her life, and each scissor cut is rugged as a bread knife... except if you were brought into the world with a straight edge in one hand and tweezers in the other, put these toolboxs on your Mother's Day list of things to get.

4. You need additional cutting mats.

Possibly not promptly, however, plan on snatching some additional mats inside a couple of months after you've gotten settled with the machine. As you begin moving into middle of the road ventures, you'll have to print on independent mats for different hues and materials, and you'll spare a ton of time by not stopping the printing while you strip vinyl from the cutting mat to make sure you can utilize it once more.

I prescribe having 3-4 standard mats and in any event 2 of the solid and fragile hold mats. By keeping extra close by, you can stack them all up before you hit print and simply move directly on through.

5. Settle on removable vinyl from the outset.

Managing vinyl as a novice takes a tad of time to become acclimated to. You will have stumbles, you will lose it, and you're going to tear a couple of lines. By beginning with removable vinyl, you can get your feet wet without the changeless duty.

When you've aced the removable vinyl ventures, then you get your young lady socks on and begin putting a lasting stamp on your reality.

6. Weeding is addictive!

You're going to end up making more activities because weeding is so unwinding. While it's an aptitude that takes practice, it truly is a pleasant method to relax and de-stress. It resembles the game Operation without the irritating ringer.

If you become as fixated on weeding as I do, here are three Design Space textual styles that require a ton of it:

For an exemplary look: CASTELLAR

For a fun vibe: CHEERFUL SHAPES

For a cutting edge feel: ITC RENNIE MACKINTOSH COM LIGHT

Also, certainly snatch a BrightPad. It'll make weeding considerably progressively fun.

7. The Maker accomplishes something beyond cutting and scoring.

One of my preferred highlights of the Cricut Maker is that it will compose with markers the very same path as it cuts. That implies if you have not-so-extraordinary penmanship, but rather you truly need to make a carefully assembled Mother's Day card, you can, in any case, draw off that adorable written by hand textual style without taking a Scripting class first.

Cricut sells a gigantic arrangement of vivid pens and markers, and you should simply pop them into the pen holder, set up your design in Design Space, and have it set as Draw rather than Cut. Inside minutes, you have yourself an expert looking composed text style for any venture you'd like. I cherish utilizing the Draw include for exceptional cards, party solicitations, place cards, school undertakings, and folio covers.

8. Design Space has Licensed Brands!

This is such a great reward for all your up and coming activities. Beside all the cool layouts and premade ventures accessible in Design Space, you can likewise cut or draw your children's preferred characters. From Star Wars to Marvel to Disney, thus significantly more, you can deck out your child's garments, room, and school supplies in their preferred TV BFFs.

My child, as of late, had medical procedure to evacuate his addendum and needed to wear a band around his midsection for over a month during his recuperation. He was extremely self-concious about wearing the band to class because he said it looked "so imbecilic." To enable him to rest easy thinking about his restorative band, we broke out the Cricut Maker and the Easy Press 2, printed out some sweet Star Wars vinyls and pressed them on. He was promptly infatuated with his new band design and was more certain than any other time in recent memory when he returned to class.

9. You children will need to utilize it the same amount of as you will.

From the minute I unpacked my Cricut Maker, my child was at that point concocting every one of the things he was going to make with it. We viewed the instructional exercise recordings together, adapted together, and conceptualized all that we could stick a vinyl mark on. Truly, this was actually "my toy," yet I LOVE the way the Maker has roused him to tune into his innovative personality and art up new things he can make, as well.

If you have more seasoned children, I certainly prescribe giving them a chance to figure out how to utilize the Maker as you realize, that way you both keep each other propelled and roused to utilize your new venture and not let it threaten you. Some incredible starter ventures for children are printing iron-ons for apparel and rucksacks, room association marks, folio covers, and paper-making ventures. You can discover a great deal of these in Design Space that are now made for you.

10. Your first task may come up short.

I set this in last because I realize you're threatened. You opened the crate, you viewed the recordings, you purchased the adornments, and!

WHAT YOU NEED TO CREATE A MAKE IT NOW CRICUT PROJECT:

Cricut Explore Air 2 (clearly)

Cricut Design Space™

Cricut Access Premium (for specific designs-some are free)

Cricut Stylus Tool

Cutting Mat

Scrapbook Paper

Tombow Aqua Liquid Glue

FOR THE BOX:

To begin with, Create a New Project in Cricut Design Space™. When you're in the new venture, select Insert Images.

Type BOX in the pursuit bar and select the picture you might want, then snap INSERT IMAGES.

Resize the picture to the size you might want.

Press GO.

Before you cut, embed the Cricut Stylus Tool into the "A" side of the cut apparatus and snap it in.

Press Go once more, place the Scrapbook Paper on the tangle, then press the stacking catch. Once the "C" catch is flickering, press it. The Cricut will consequently score, then cut the picture.

Overlap along all the score lines, and Glue the fold as an afterthought to within the case.

FOR THE FLOWER:

Make another task or erase the case from your page.

Go to CARTRIDGES, then look down until you see 3D FLORAL HOME DECOR, then snap on VIEW ALL IMAGES.

Select the blossom you might want to make (you can see the one I picked featured in green in the pictures above), then select the INSERT IMAGES catch in the lower right corner.

Resize the picture (they're associated, so they'll resize by and large). As should be obvious, there are 3 different hues. These organize with the different paper you will use for every one. So you'll be stacking three different shading decisions when you send it to the Cricut.

Select GO.

It will initially cut the leaves, so place the Scrapbook Paper you might want to use for the leaf shading on the tangle. Select GO once more, then burden the tangle it into the Cricut.

When the "C" catch flashes, push it, and the Cricut will begin cutting. When completed, expel the paper from the tangle.

Rehash stages 5 through 7 with the petals, and pick a different paper.

Rehash stages 5 through 7 with the polished product.

Twist every one of the petals, then Glue everything together.

CRICUT ACCESSORIES AND SUPPLIES – THE MOST USEFUL

Hoping to make with a Cricut Explore Air, however, don't have the foggiest idea where to begin? I've recorded the MOST Useful Cricut extras and supplies so you can begin making!

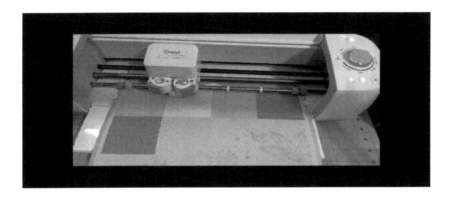

This likely won't be a stun to anybody, yet I will uncover it in any case. I crowd specialty supplies. I have an entire storage room brimming with things I haven't utilized in about a year, and consistently I state I'll get it out tomorrow and it never completes. So now, when I head to the specialty store, I just purchase the fundamentals. My office makeover is near being done, so I need to keep it clean for until the end of time. So when I state these are the most helpful Cricut frill and supplies, I imply that I keep these things convenient consistently.

I utilize the vast majority of these Cricut supplies on a week by week, if not regular schedule. Other than my specialty supplies, my Cricut Explore Air gets the most use in my office. I'm going to separate this into two sections for you to make it simpler to explore. One area is my preferred supplies and materials, and the other is the Cricut embellishments and instruments that I can't survive without!

To make sure you know... A LOT of the items I'm referencing are in the

Here is a helpful rundown of Cricut adornments and supplies, and beneath I'll separate them for you.

THE MOST USEFUL CRICUT ACCESSORIES AND MATERIALS TO GET STARTED:

Cricut Pens

Indoor Removeable Vinyl

Cement Foil

Iron-On Vinyl

Move Tape

Printable Materials

Cardstock

Cricut Pens are extremely fun and simple to utilize. I use them to make Hand Lettering Projects.

Indoor Removeable Vinyl is extraordinary for any home style DIY venture. I made this Gold Foil Teepee with the Adhesive Foil (which is basically vinyl), and I'll be posting about my vinyl divider instructional exercise soon! You can likewise utilize vinyl as a stencil to make PERFECT hand-lettered workmanship. For these ventures, ensure you get some Transfer Tape.

Obviously, I can't make this rundown without referencing some Printable Materials and Cardstock! You'll discover everything from Printable texture to Printable Iron On. Utilize the cardstock to print out your very own designs like this charming Unicorn Printable, or make Paper Flowers with the designed cardstock.

Talking about Iron-On Vinyl, I'm enamored with the Glitter Iron-On (see the instructional exercise for utilizing it HERE). Obviously, there are numerous materials to look over, similar to thwart and neon!

If you're getting down to business with vinyl, you NEED this Weeder apparatus. You use it to pick the abundance vinyl away. See it being used HERE.

The X-Large Scraper is my preferred instrument to utilize. I use it to smooth down paper or vinyl to the tangle or to scratch off material that adheres to the tangle. The Small Scraper and Spatula set is additionally extremely helpful.

I utilize different tangles for specific materials. Since I don't need the cardstock to stick excessively, I utilize the Light Grip Mat for printables. The Strong Grip Mat is ideal for thicker things like Glitter Iron-On, and I utilize the Standard tangle for most different things. Buy the Cutting Mat Set at first, then buy the individual mats when you have to supplant them. I likewise prefer to utilize the 12X24" Mat Set for huge vinyl ventures.

Ensure you likewise get some Extra Blades, and the Deep Cut Blade is convenient for thicker things like chipboard.

CRICUT MACHINE TROUBLESHOOTING TIPS

Is it true that you are having Cricut Design Space issues?

Is it stacking gradually, solidifying inside and out, slamming, or not opening by any stretch of the imagination? It's so baffling when this occurs, because you simply need to continue ahead with your task, isn't that so? I know how it feels, and in this post I'm going to give you a couple of tips on what to do about these Design Space issues.

Step by step instructions to Fix Cricut Design Space Problems

Generally, Design Space is an awesome programming. Truly, there are a couple of more highlights we'd like to see included (was extraordinary to get a bended book highlight as of late), however in general it functions admirably for generally extends. The most serious issue is smashing, slow stacking, solidifying, or not opening. We should investigate what you may have the option to do to fix these issues.

Machine

My machine isn't cutting my material:

- Check the tenacity of your tangle

- Check that you are utilizing the right hued tangle for the material you are cutting

- Clean your edge; check for any garbage that might be gotten around the cutting edge tip

- Use a wad of foil to hone your edge, by cutting it on different occasions. If this doesn't work, you may need to think about another edge

- Check that you have the right setting for the material you are cutting

- Increase the edge weight by changing the material setting

- Increase the picture size , the picture possibly too little and perplexing

- For many-sided cuts on card, utilize the mind boggling cut card setting

The power button on my machine is red:

Glimmering Red Light

- Check for a firmware update

Strong red light

- Turn off the machine, and unplug for two or three minutes before connecting back, and fueling on

- Check Machine for garbage and residue

- Move carriage to and fro in any event multiple times

- Check, and change, the power source

- Call Cricut support if the issue endures

Print and cut

My machine isn't enlisting the print and cut imprints:

- Make sure the machine is in shade, brilliant daylight prevents the sensor from getting the lines, If this doesn't work it may be that your room is excessively dull! Have a go at sparkling a light onto the sensor.

- The Explore Air Machines can just enroll white cardstock, The Maker anyway can identify print and cut lines on shaded and Kraft card

- Go over the dark lines with a dark sharpie, to enable your machine to get the line.

Print and cut isn't cutting precisely:

- Re-align your machine

- Check if drain has been empowered

Mats

My mats are never again clingy:

- Wash with cleaning up fluid, tenderly scouring into the tangle surface, flush in warm water and leave to air dry

- Designate tangles for specific materials

- Buy another tangle!

The material is tearing when I expel it from the tangle:

- Turn over the tangle, and strip the tangle away from the material

- Check that you are utilizing the correct hued tangle for the correct sort of material

- On first tangle use, press the tangle against a bit of attire to dispose of a little tenacity

Simple Press

My vinyl isn't following great when utilizing my simple press:

- Check that the surface you are going ahead is tough

- Always utilize the Easy Press tangle

- Check the right temperature, and time, for your material and vinyl on the online Easy Press control - https://cricut.com/heatguide

- Check the strip off temperature for the vinyl you are utilizing

Devices

Knife Blade:

My picture isn't cutting with the Knife Blade:

- Check the picture size, inside cuts ought to be no littler than ¾ of an inch

- Check the thickness of lines, these ought to be in any event as thick as the finish of a standard pencil

- Only utilize the knife sharp edge when your machine is associated by means of the USB link, never Bluetooth and that you have a solid Wi-Fi association

- Ensure the material is taped down on every one of the four sides

I'm experiencing difficulty cutting chipboard:

- Leave your chipboard out of its bundling for at any rate 24hours before cutting

Knife sharp edge is doing such a large number of goes and slicing through my tangle:

- Pause undertaking and check after a couple of spends, in some cases the knife edge will have totally sliced through the material before it has completed the process of cutting. If this is the situation, delay then launch your venture

- Change the measure of passes

Knife sharp edge isn't slicing through my material:

- Check material settings

- Add extra passes

Scoring Tools

My machine naturally picks the scoring wheel for scoring, however I have the scoring stylus:

- Click alter apparatuses eager for advancement it screen, and pick the scoring stylus

How would I change the scoring tip on the scoring wheel?

- Press the catch over the scoring wheel to discharge the tip

Configuration Space

Configuration space is 'glitchy':

- Check for programming refreshes, and download likewise

- Change programs

- Check web association

How would I interface with Bluetooth?

- Enable Bluetooth on the gadget you might want to interface your machine to

- Select your machine and enter secret word 0000

- Explore and Explore Air machines need a Bluetooth connector to interface with a Bluetooth empowered gadget

Configuration space is charging me for pictures I have just bought/I'm bought in to Cricut get to, and I'm being charged for access pictures:

- Log out and log back in to your record, plan space will once in a while sign you out without you understanding

Step by step instructions to Fix Cricut Design Space Problems

Generally, Design Space is an awesome programming. Indeed, there are a couple of more highlights we'd like to see included (was extraordinary to get a bended book highlight as of late), however all in all it functions admirably for generally extends.

The most concerning issue is smashing, slow stacking, solidifying, or not opening. How about we investigate what you may have the option to do to fix these issues.

1. Slow Internet Connection

The primary driver of issues with Design Space is a moderate web association. The program requires great and reliable transfer and download speeds. A conflicting association with plunges and spikes may likewise mess up the product. You'll likely get an increasingly reliable association if your gadget is nearer to your modem.

Destinations like YouTube require great download velocities and you can pull off a more slow transfer speed. However, Cricut Design Space requires both download and transfer rates to be great, as you are continually sending and accepting data as you chip away at your plan.

Run A Speed Test

Run a web speed test with an assistance like Ookla.

Cricut specifies the accompanying prerequisites for Design Space to run well:

Broadband association

Minimum 2 – 3 Mbps Download

Least 1 – 2 Mbps Upload

If your outcomes are extremely low, and you feel that is causing or adding to your issues, call your network access supplier. It may be that you need another modem to give the necessary rates. That was my concern a year or two prior. Another modem completely tackled my issues – it's only an agony holding up a couple of days!

2. Your Computer

If it's not your web speed, the issue might be the PC, tablet, or cell phone that you are utilizing. There are prescribed least necessities for Design Space to run well. Here are the nuts and bolts:

Windows Computers

Your Windows PC should:

- be running on Windows 8 or later
- have Intel Core arrangement or AMD processor – mine has AMD and runs extraordinary
- have 4GB of Ram
- at any rate 50MB of free plate space – the more the better
- have a free USB port or bluetooth association

Macintosh Computers

Your Mac PC will require the accompanying for Design Space to work:

- the Mac OS X 10.12 or something later
- a CPU of 1.83 GHz
- have 4GB Ram
- have 50MB free space
- an accessible USB port or bluetooth capacities.

Foundation Programs

Another issue might be an excess of foundation projects running while you are attempting to utilize Design Space.

It is safe to say that you are at the same time watching Netflix, talking on Facebook, Skyping your mother, downloading the last period of Fixer Upper, transferring your most recent Vlog to YouTube, all while attempting to structure a tee in Design Space? All things considered, other than meriting an award for having the option to achieve such a great amount without a moment's delay, you'll have to close a couple of projects to get DS moving easily.

However, all joking aside, it may be the issue, regardless of whether you're not doing all that. In some cases simply shutting the things you're not utilizing will speed things up.

Different Things That Might Help

Here are a couple of different things you may jump at the chance to test out or complete:

- clearing your store and history
- check what your enemy of infection programming is doing and update if vital
- update drivers (for Windows)
- defragment your hard drive
- run a malware check

These tests will help speed your PC up or may tackle the issue all together.

3. Your Browser

Another conceivable reason for your Design Space issues could be your program.

Cricut specifies you should utilize the most recent variant of a specific program. Regardless of whether you use Chrome, Mozilla, Firefox, or Edge, guarantee it is modern. If one program isn't working, check if it works in another. Now and then, for no good reason, this can take care of the issue.

4. Call Cricut

When all else fizzles, you may need to call Cricut client care to examine your specific issue.

I know there will be a lot of issues that stay unaddressed here, so please leave a remark with what your battle is and another person may have the option to support you!

My machine is making a surprising commotion (Older Machines)

Applies to Cricut Personal, Cricut Create, Cricut Cake, Cricut Cake Mini, Cricut Expression, Cricut Expression 2, and Cricut Imagine.

No one enjoys an uproarious machine. If your Cricut machine causes an irregular commotion, to please choose your machine from the connections underneath and pursue the showed steps to investigate the issue:

Cricut Expression 2

Cricut Imagine

Cricut Personal, Cricut Create, Cricut Cake, Cricut Cake Mini, Cricut Expression

Cricut Expression 2

A shrill grinding sound when carriage vehicle moves

Uproarious clamor when stacking the tangle

Uproarious clamor upon startup

A shrill grinding sound when carriage vehicle moves

Complete a visual review of the machine. If any of coming up next are off, or not working appropriately, kindly contact Member Care for further help:

Are the roller bars adjusted and rolling appropriately?

Is the belt tight?

Move the carriage vehicle somewhat to one side and ensure the wheels on the two sides are on the track.

Uproarious clamor when stacking the tangle

Guarantee that you are utilizing the right size of mats for your machine.

Guarantee that the tangle is stacked utilizing the tangle stacking guides. The tangle should be embedded under these aides so as to stack appropriately.

Have a go at moving your machine to a different surface and burden the tangle once more. If the machine isn't completely upheld, or the surface is uneven, this can cause the stacking activity to skew, bringing about abnormal commotion.

If you are utilizing the right tangles, have stacked it utilizing the aides, moved the machine to a different surface and the clamor is as yet occurring, take a concise video of the issue and contact Member Care. The operator will give directions to present your video and will help you further.

Boisterous clamor upon startup

Complete a visual examination of the machine. If any of coming up next are off, or not working appropriately, it would be ideal if you contact Member Care for further help:

Are the roller bars adjusted and rolling appropriately?

Is the belt tight?

Move the carriage vehicle somewhat to one side and ensure the wheels on the two sides are on the track.

Cricut Imagine

Dull humming clamor when attempting to fire up

Contact Member Care through one of the choices underneath for further help.

Cricut Personal, Cricut Create, Cricut Cake, Cricut Cake Mini, Cricut Expression

Clamor during the cut procedure

Commotion when firing up

Commotion during the cut procedure

For help deciding whether the clamor you are hearing is bizarre for your machine, if you don't mind contact Member Care. If calling, the specialist can tune in to the commotion through the telephone line and let you know. You can likewise take a concise video when the clamor is happening, and after that contact Member Care through any of the choices underneath. The specialist will give you guidelines about how to present the video, and help you further.

Play out a visual assessment to decide whether physical harm could be causing the commotion the machine makes during cutting:

Is the carriage vehicle on the track and straight?

Is the belt free or broken?

If the carriage vehicle or the belt/track are warped, free or broken, take a concise video when the commotion is happening, and after that contact Member Care through any of the choices underneath. The specialist will give you guidelines about how to present the video, and help you further.

Guarantee that the tangle was agreed with the tangle manages on the machine and stacked straight. If the tangle is slanted to one side or the right, it can rub on the mass of the machine during cutting and cause the clamor.

If the machine keeps on causing commotion during cutting, to please contact Member Care through one of the choices underneath for further help.

Clamor when firing up

Guarantee that all cardboard bundling has been expelled from around the carriage vehicle.

Play out a visual review to decide whether physical harm could be causing the clamor the machine makes during cutting:

Is the carriage vehicle on the track and straight?

Is the belt free or broken?

If the carriage vehicle or the belt/track are screwy, free or broken, take a concise video when the clamor is happening, and after that contact Member Care through any of the choices beneath. The operator will give you directions about how to present the video, and help you further.

Contact Member Care for help deciding whether the clamor you are hearing is uncommon for your machine. If calling, the specialist can tune in to the clamor through the telephone line and let you know. You can likewise take a concise video when the clamor is happening, and afterward contact Member Care through any of the alternatives underneath. The operator will give you guidelines about how to present the video, and help you further.

Machine isn't slicing through my material (Older Machines)

Applies to Cricut Personal, Cricut Create, Cricut Cake, Cricut Cake Mini, Cricut Expression, Cricut Expression 2, Cricut Imagine.

If your Cricut machine isn't carving right through your material or is just scoring the material, this issue can typically be settled with some fundamental investigating.

Cricut Personal, Cricut Create, Cricut Cake, Cricut Cake Mini, Cricut Expression

Guarantee that you are utilizing the right cut settings.

Expel the sharp edge lodging. Guarantee that you are utilizing a Cricut brand sharp edge. Then examine the sharp edge and edge lodging and evacuate any garbage that might be adhered to the cutting edge or held up in the edge lodging. Make a point to supplant the sharp edge lodging once again into your machine effectively. When clean, play out a test cut. If the edge and lodging were at that point free from garbage or cleaning didn't help, continue to stage 3.

Attempt an arm lightness test: delicately press down on the dark arms that encompass the sharp edge lodging and after that discharge them. Do they bob right back up, or do they stick or rub in any capacity? If they stick or rub, it would be ideal if you contact Member Care through one of the alternatives underneath for further help. If they bob right back up when discharged, continue to stage 4.

Increment the machine weight setting and attempt a test cut. If this doesn't change the cut outcome, continue to stage 5.

Increment sharp edge profundity by turning the dial at the highest point of your cutting edge lodging. If this doesn't change the cut outcome, continue to stage 6.

Play out a hard reset on the machine.

Retry your cuts with another sharp edge lodging.

If the machine is as yet not slicing through materials or is just scoring the paper, if it's not too much trouble contact Member Care through one of the alternatives underneath for further help.

Cricut Expression 2, Imagine

Expel the cutting edge lodging. Guarantee you are utilizing a Cricut brand cutting edge. Then assess the sharp edge and edge lodging and evacuate any flotsam and jetsam that might be adhered to the edge or stopped in the cutting edge lodging.

Try to supplant the sharp edge lodging once again into your machine effectively. If the cutting edge and lodging were at that point free from flotsam and jetsam, continue to stage 3.

Increment machine weight settings, which are situated in the Project Preview screen, and attempt a test cut. If this doesn't change the outcome, continue to stage 4.

Increment cutting edge profundity by turning the dial on the edge lodging and attempt a test cut. If this doesn't change the cut outcome, continue to stage 5.

Attempt an arm lightness test: tenderly press down on the dark arms that encompass the cutting edge lodging and afterward discharge them. Do they ricochet right back up or do they stick or rub in any capacity? If they stick or rub, it would be ideal if you contact Member Care through one of the alternatives beneath for further help. If they ricochet right back up when discharged, continue to stage 6.

Attempt a test cut with another sharp edge lodging.

My machine is tearing or hauling through my material (Older Machines)

There are a few factors that may make a machine tear through material. Luckily, this issue can more often than not be settled with some essential investigating steps. If your Cricut machine is tearing or hauling through the material, check the accompanying:

Cricut Personal, Cricut Create, Cricut Cake, Cricut Cake Mini, Cricut Expression

Play out a Hard Reset on the machine. If this doesn't help, continue to 2.

If the edge is as yet hauling through your material, it would be ideal if you contact Member Care through one of the choices beneath for further help.

Cricut Expression 2, Cricut Imagine

Expel the edge lodging from the machine, then evacuate the cutting edge and check for any flotsam and jetsam inside the lodging or on the sharp edge.

Guarantee that you supplant the cutting edge lodging into the machine accurately. If you didn't discover trash adhered to the sharp edge or stopped inside the lodging, continue to stage 3.

Increment machine weight settings, situated on the Project Preview screen. If this doesn't change the outcome, continue to stage 4.

Increment sharp edge profundity by turning the dial on the edge lodging. If this doesn't change the outcome, continue to stage 5.

Attempt an arm lightness test. Delicately press down on the dark arms that encompass the cutting edge lodging and after that discharge them. They should ricochet right back up If they stick or rub in any capacity, if it's not too much trouble contact Member Care through one of the alternatives beneath for further help. If they skip right back up when discharged, continue to stage 6.

Retry your cuts with sharp edge lodging. If the issue endures, kindly contact Member Care through one of the choices underneath for help.

Machine entryway issues (Older Machines)

Applies to Cricut Personal, Cricut Create, Cricut Cake, Cricut Cake Mini, Cricut Expression

Entryways won't open/remain open

Guarantee the sticker that covers the entryway has been expelled. This sticker is clear with words on it and strips off effectively

Tenderly yet immovably endeavor to pry the entryways open. In some cases it takes a couple of times opening and shutting the ways to break them in.

If the entryways still won't open, if you don't mind contact Member Care through one of the choices underneath for further help.

Entryways won't close/remain shut

Ensure that you are first shutting the base entryway and after that the top entryway, applying enough manual strain to tap the entryways set up. Now and again it takes a couple of times opening and shutting the ways to "break them in."

If the entryways still won't close or remain shut, if it's not too much trouble contact Member Care through one of the choices beneath for further help.

Cricut Expression 2 - Light Issues

Cutting light doesn't mood killer

Go to Machine Settings and change the Cutting Light to "During Cutting" or "Constantly Off," and afterward press "Spare".

If the machine light still doesn't mood killer, if you don't mind contact Member Care through one of the choices underneath for further help.

Cutting light doesn't turn On

Go to Machine Settings and change the Cutting Light to "During Cutting" or "Consistently On," and afterward press "Spare".

If the light doesn't come on when the setting has been changed, or the LED bulb is broken, if it's not too much trouble contact Member Care through one of the alternatives underneath for help.

If the light comes on when the settings have been changed, this affirms the light works, and a constrained firmware update is required. Be that as it may, firmware refreshes for Cricut Expression 2 are never again conceivable. It would be ideal if you contact Member Care through one of the choices underneath for further help.

Cricut machine power issues (more seasoned machines)

If you are encountering issues with capacity to your Cricut machine, if you don't mind select your machine from the connections beneath and pursue the prescribed investigating steps.

Cricut Expression 2

Cricut Imagine

Cricut Gypsy

Cricut Personal, Cricut Create, Cricut Cake, Cricut Cake Mini, Cricut Expression

Cricut Expression 2

Continues turning to the Welcome Screen as well as restarting

Machine won't control on

Continues turning to the Welcome Screen as well as restarting

Contact Member Care through one of the alternatives underneath for further help.

Machine won't control on

Guarantee that the attachment is secure in the power port on the machine, in the power connector, and in the divider outlet. If the string is safely embedded at all focuses, continue to stage 2.

Have a go at interfacing the power rope to a different divider outlet. If this doesn't resolve the issue, continue to stage 3.

Check the power connector in the power string, and ensure that the green light on the crate is lit up. If it isn't lit up, the string should be supplanted. If the light on the container is lit up, contact Member Care through one of the alternatives beneath for further help.

Cricut Imagine

The machine won't control on

Guarantee that the attachment is secure in the power port on the machine, in the power connector, and in the divider outlet. If the string is safely embedded at all focuses, continue to stage 2.

Have a go at interfacing the power rope to a different divider outlet. If this doesn't resolve the issue, continue to stage 3.

Check the power connector in the power string, and ensure that the green light on the crate is lit up. If it isn't lit up, it would be ideal if you contact Member Care through one of the alternatives underneath for further help.

Cricut Gypsy

Wanderer power port has broken

Vagabond won't hold a charge

Vagabond won't control on/close off out of the blue

Tramp power port has broken

If the power port on the Gypsy is broken, a fix is the main arrangement.

As of now, be that as it may, Gypsy fixes are not accessible because of an absence of stockpile of the parts expected to fix the machines.

If you have to uplink the cartridges on it to your Cricut represent use with your Explore or Maker machine, if it's not too much trouble contact Member Care through one the alternatives underneath for help.

Rover won't hold a charge

Associate your Gypsy to the power supply. The machine should control on, however give a red light; this equitable shows that it should be charged. If it won't hold an accuse of the present power rope and outlet, continue to stage 2.

Take a stab at interfacing the power rope to a different electrical plug and attempt to charge the Gypsy. If it doesn't hold a charge subsequent to charging in the new outlet, continue to stage 3.

Attempt a different power rope. If you don't have another Gypsy power line to attempt, it would be ideal if you contact Member Care through one of the alternatives beneath for help.

If attempting another power rope doesn't help, continue to stage 4.

A charging port fix, which incorporates another battery, is required. Be that as it may, Gypsy fixes are never again accessible because of an absence of stockpile of the parts expected to fix the machines. If you have to fix the Gypsy so you can uplink the cartridges on it to your Cricut represent use with your Explore or Maker machine, if it's not too much trouble contact Member Care through one the choices underneath for help.

Vagabond won't control on/stop out of the blue

Interface your Gypsy to the power supply. The machine should control on, however give a red light; this equitable demonstrates that it should be charged. Charge it for some time. Then, if it will at present not control on, or close off surprisingly, continue to stage 2.

Take a stab at associating the power string to a different electrical plug and attempt to charge the Gypsy. If it will at present not control on, or close off out of the blue, continue to stage 3.

Attempt a different power rope. If you don't have another Gypsy power string to attempt, kindly contact Member Care through one of the choices underneath for help. If attempting another power rope doesn't help, continue to stage 4.

Another battery and potentially a charging port fix, which incorporates another battery, is required. Be that as it may, Gypsy fixes are never again accessible because of an absence of stock of the parts expected to fix the machines. If you have to uplink the cartridges on it to your Cricut represent use with your Explore or Maker machine, it would be ideal if you contact Member Care through one the choices underneath for help.

Cricut Personal, Cricut Create, Cricut Cake, Cricut Cake Mini, Cricut Expression

The machine is getting power however doesn't fire up (roller bars don't move)

The machine won't control on

The machine won't remain fueled on

The machine is getting power however doesn't fire up (roller bars don't move)

Decide whether the machine is in "Firmware Mode." When the Power button, Cut catch, and fastens on the left of the keypad are lit up, this implies the Cricut might be in Firmware Mode. Play out a Hard Reset on the machine.

If stages 2 doesn't resolve the issue, if it's not too much trouble contact Member Care through one of the alternatives underneath for further help.

The machine won't control on

Guarantee that the fitting is secure in the power port on the machine, in the power connector, and in the divider outlet. If the line is safely embedded at all focuses, continue to stage 2.

Check the power connector in the power line, and ensure that the green light on the case is lit up. If it isn't lit up, the string should be supplanted. If the light on the crate is lit up, continue to stage 3.

Have a go at interfacing the power string to a different divider outlet. If this doesn't resolve the issue, continue to stage 4.

Take a stab at utilizing another power rope in the event that there is an issue with your present power line.

If the new power string doesn't resolve the issue, it would be ideal if you contact Member Care through one of the alternatives beneath for further help.

The machine won't remain controlled on

Guarantee that the attachment is secure in the power port on the machine, in the power connector, and in the divider outlet. If the line is safely embedded at all focuses, continue to stage 2.

Check the power connector in the power rope, and ensure that the green light on the case is lit up. If it isn't lit up, the string should be supplanted. If the light on the crate is lit up, continue to stage 3.

Take a stab at associating the power rope to a different divider outlet. If this doesn't resolve the issue, continue to stage 4.

Offer the Cricut a reprieve; turn it off and enable it to rest for around 10 minutes every hour. If this doesn't help, continue to stage 5.

Have a go at utilizing another power line on the off chance that there is an issue with your present power string.

If the new power string doesn't resolve the issue, if it's not too much trouble contact Member Care through one of the choices beneath for further help.

Cricut machine roller bars are not moving (more seasoned machines)

If the roller bars on your Cricut machine don't roll when controlling the machine on or squeezing the heap tangle button, it would be ideal if you pursue the suggested investigating steps:

Material for:

Cricut Personal

Cricut Create

Cricut Cake/Cake Mini

Cricut Expression

Roller Bars Won't Roll on Startup

Decide whether the roller bar is free, harmed, or uneven. If it is, snap a picture or short video of the harm and contact Member Care through one of the choices beneath for further help.

Decide whether the machine is in "Firmware Mode." When the Power button, Cut catch, and fastens on the left of the keypad are lit up, this implies the Cricut might be in Firmware Mode. Play out a Hard Reset on the machine.

If the roller bar isn't free, harmed, or uneven, and the Hard Reset doesn't help, if it's not too much trouble contact Member Care through one of the alternatives beneath for further help.

Roller Bars Won't Roll When Loading the Mat

Decide whether the roller bar is free, harmed, or uneven. If it is, snap a picture or short video of the harm and contact Member Care through one of the choices underneath for further help.

Guarantee that a cartridge is stacked in the machine. The Load Mat catch may not work if a cartridge isn't stacked.

Press the Unload Mat catch and afterward press the Load Mat catch once more. The Cricut machine may believe that a cutting mat is now stacked in the machine.

Press the Reset All catch to clear all directions and afterward press the Load Mat catch once more.

Have a go at utilizing a different cartridge. If the roller bar will move with a different cartridge, it would be ideal if you contact Member Care through one of the choices beneath for further help.

Play out a Hard Reset on the machine.

If the roller bars still won't roll when stacking the tangle, if you don't mind contact Member Care through one of the alternatives beneath for further help.

My machine signals twice when I endeavor to place it into Firmware Update mode

Applies to: Cricut Personal, Cricut Create, Cricut Cake, Cricut Cake Mini, Cricut Expression.

If you have to refresh your machine's firmware, yet it is signaling twice when you endeavor to place it into firmware update mode, if it's not too much trouble contact Member Care through one of the alternatives beneath for help.

My Cricut screen is showing an inappropriate cartridge name

If the screen on your Cricut Personal Cutter, Create, Cake, Cake Mini, or Expression machine is showing an inappropriate cartridge name when a cartridge is embedded, pursue the prescribed investigating ventures beneath:

Evacuate the cartridge and set it back in reverse. It is conceivable that the stickers were inappropriately set on the cartridge.

Does the screen demonstrate the wrong cartridge name with the majority of your cartridges?

Indeed: continue to 3.

No: If the issue is with only one cartridge, and the Cricut is as yet demonstrating the wrong cartridge name in the wake of placing it in reverse, contact Member Care.

Play out a Hard Reset on the machine.

If the Cricut screen keeps on demonstrating the off base cartridge name with your cartridges, kindly contact Member Care for further help.

Cricut machine dials are not working

Material for:

Cricut Personal

Cricut Create

Cricut Cake/Cake Mini

Cricut Expression

If you are encountering issues with the dial(s) on your Cricut machine, if it's not too much trouble pursue the prescribed investigating steps.

Is the dial broken or pushed in?

If along these lines, snap a photo of the issue and contact Member Care through one of the choices beneath for help. If the dial isn't split or pushed in, continue to 2.

Play out a Hard Reset on the machine.

My Cricut machine solidifies when I attempt to add pictures to the line

If your Cricut Personal Cutter, Create, Cake, Cake Mini, or Expression machine solidifies when you attempt to add pictures to the picture line, pursue the investigating ventures underneath.

Offer the Cricut a reprieve; turn the Cricut off and enable it to rest for around 10 minutes every hour.

Guarantee that you are entering characters in the right request and trusting that the picture will show up on the screen before entering the following character.

Tip: Remember to choose dark component keys before choosing white picture keys.

Decide what number of pictures are being added to the line.

The picture line has constrained memory and can just recollect such a large number of pictures. When you arrive at the most extreme number of pictures for the memory, you will get a blunder message that says "Characters won't fit." Simply expel pictures from the line until the message vanishes. If this doesn't resolve the issue, continue to 5.

Take a stab at utilizing a different cartridge. If the Cricut never again solidifies while including pictures with a different cartridge, contact Member Care by means of telephone or online visit for help. If the issue perseveres with different cartridges, continue to 6.

Play out a Hard Reset on the machine.

If the Cricut keeps on solidifying, if it's not too much trouble contact Member Care through telephone or online visit for further help.

My Cricut machine solidifies when I load or empty the tangle

If your Cricut Personal Cutter, Create, Cake, Cake Mini, or Expression machine solidifies when you load or empty the tangle, pursue the suggested investigating ventures underneath.

Offer the Cricut a reprieve. Turn the Cricut off and enable it to rest for around 10 minutes every hour.

Ensure you are not "hot-swapping" cartridges. "Hot-swapping" is exchanging cartridges while the Cricut is controlled On.

If solidifying during stacking as it were:

Guarantee a cartridge is stacked in the machine.

Press the Unload Mat catch and after that press the Load Mat catch once more.

Press the Reset All catch to clear all directions and after that press the Load Mat catch once more

Take a stab at utilizing a different cartridge. If the Cricut never again solidifies while stacking/emptying the tangle with a different cartridge, if it's not too much trouble contact Member Care through one of the choices beneath for further help.

Play out a Hard Reset on the machine.

My Cricut machine is cold during cutting

If your Cricut Personal Cutter, Create, Cake, Cake Mini, or Expression machine is cold up when cutting, it would be ideal if you pursue the prescribed investigating ventures beneath to determine the issue.

Offer the Cricut a reprieve. Turn the Cricut off and enable it to rest for around 10 minutes every hour.

Have a go at utilizing a different cartridge. If the Cricut never again solidifies during cutting with a different cartridge, it would be ideal if you contact Member Care through one of the alternatives underneath for further help.

Play out a Hard Reset on the machine.

The carriage of my Cricut machine doesn't move along the track when cutting

If the carriage of your Cricut Personal Cutter, Create, Cake, Cake Mini, or Expression machine doesn't move along the track during cutting, pursue the investigating ventures beneath.

With the Cricut controlled on, can you effectively pull the carriage vehicle left and right along the track? If the carriage vehicle can't be pulled along the track or won't move by any stretch of the imagination, if it's not too much trouble contact Member Care through one of the choices beneath for further help. If you can move the carriage vehicle along the track, continue to 2.

Play out a visual review of the roller bars, carriage vehicle, and belt to decide whether physical harm could be making the carriage vehicle not move.

Is the carriage vehicle on the track and straight?

Is the belt free or broken?

If the carriage vehicle or the belt/track are slanted, free or broken, snap a picture of the issue and contact Member Care through one of the choices underneath for further help.

My Cricut machine says "Characters won't fit"

If your Cricut Personal Cutter, Create, Cake, Cake Mini, or Expression machine says, "Characters won't fit," pursue the investigating ventures underneath to determine the issue.

Decide what number of pictures are being added to the line.

The picture line has restricted memory and can just recall such a large number of pictures. When you arrive at the most extreme number of pictures for the memory, you will get a mistake message that says "Characters won't fit." Simply expel pictures from the line until the message vanishes. If this doesn't resolve the issue, continue to 2.

Decide the size of the picture to be cut. Not all pictures can be cut at all size choices for each machine. This is because of the manner in which pictures are proportioned and set on the tangle by the machine: the size dial sets the stature, yet the picture is set width-wise on the tangle, with the goal that the highest point of the picture is at the privilege of the tangle, and the base of the picture is at the left of the tangle. Thusly a few pictures, at the biggest size, are too tall to even think about fitting on the tangle left to right.

Have a go at utilizing the paper saver highlight to help pictures fit better on the tangle, or abatement the picture size until it fits on the tangle. If this doesn't resolve the issue, continue to 3.

If you have another Cricut machine that can be utilized independent, endeavor to copy the issue by cutting a similar picture at a similar size on a similar kind of machine. If the picture won't cut on that machine either, and gives you a similar blunder message, then the picture is simply unreasonably huge for the machine/tangle. If you don't have another Cricut machine on which to attempt this, contact Member Care through one of the choices beneath; they can endeavor the cut and help analyze the issue. If the cut on a different machine is fruitful, continue to 4.

Play out a Hard Reset on the machine.

There are issues with the catches on my Cricut Machine keypad

If there are issues with the catches on your Cricut machine's keypad, select the mistake from the connections underneath and pursue the prescribed investigating steps.

Applies to: Cricut Personal, Cricut Create, Cricut Cake, Cricut Cake Mini, Cricut Expression

The catches on my keypad don't react when chosen

A portion of the lights on my keypad are lit up, yet none of the catches will react

The catches on my keypad don't react when chosen

Guarantee that a cartridge is stacked into the machine and that the machine has perceived that a cartridge is stacked (the name of the cartridge will show up on the screen), as certain catches are not actuated except if a cartridge has been stacked into the machine. If there is as of now a cartridge in the machine and it is being perceived by the machine, continue to 2.

Guarantee that the cutting mat has been stacked into the machine. A few catches are not enacted except if a tangle is stacked into the machine.

Take a stab at utilizing a different cartridge. If the keypad catches react with a different cartridge, contact Member Care through one of the alternatives underneath for further help. If the catch still doesn't react with different cartridges, continue to 4.

Play out a Hard Reset on the machine.

If the keypad fastens still don't react, it would be ideal if you contact Member Care through one of the alternatives underneath for further help.

A portion of the lights on my keypad are lit up, however none of the catches will react

When the Power button, Cut catch, and fastens on the left of the keypad are lit up, this implies the Cricut might be in Firmware Mode (for the Personal/V1, simply the power catch and cut catch).

There is an issue with my Cricut machine's screen

This assistance book covers potential Cricut machine screen issues. If you're encountering issues with your screen, if it's not too much trouble select your machine in one the connections beneath and pursue the proposed investigating steps.

Cricut Personal, Cricut Create, Cricut Cake, Cricut Cake Mini, Cricut Expression

Cricut Expression 2

Cricut Imagine

Cricut Gypsy

Cricut Personal, Cricut Create, Cricut Cake, Cricut Cake Mini, Cricut Expression

The showcase is indicating boxes

The screen is clear/doesn't indicate anything

Note: A firmware update is the investigating for the issues above. In any case, we never again can perform Firmware Updates for the machines recorded previously. Kindly contact Member Care for any help.

Cricut Expression 2

Stuck on the Welcome Screen

Continues turning to the Welcome Screen as well as restarting

LCD is lethargic

Stuck on the End User License Agreement (EULA)

LCD Calibration is off

Adhered on the Tap to Zoom/Icon Label message

The showcase is white, hazy, or pixelated

Tangle review demonstrates a dim box

Stuck on Welcome Screen

Contact Member Care through one of the choices beneath for further help.

Continues turning to the Welcome Screen or potentially restarting

Contact Member Care through one of the choices beneath for further help.

LCD is lethargic

Guarantee that the silicone defensive spread has been evacuated.

Power off the machine and play out a Hard Reset on the machine.

If the screen is as yet lethargic after the Hard Reset, if it's not too much trouble contact Member Care through one of the choices underneath for further help.

Stuck on the End User License Agreement (EULA)

Guarantee that the silicone defensive spread has been expelled.

Power off the machine and play out a Hard Reset on the machine.

If the Hard Reset doesn't help, it would be ideal if you contact Member Care through one of the choices beneath for further help.

LCD Calibration is off

Guarantee that the silicone defensive spread has been evacuated.

Power off the machine and play out a Hard Reset on the machine.

If the Hard Reset doesn't help, if it's not too much trouble contact Member Care through one of the choices beneath for further help.

Adhered on the Tap to Zoom/Icon Label message

Guarantee that the silicone defensive spread has been evacuated.

Power off the machine and play out a Hard Reset on the machine.

If the Hard Reset doesn't help, if it's not too much trouble contact Member Care through one of the choices underneath for further help.

The presentation is white, hazy, or pixelated

Guarantee that the silicone defensive spread has been expelled.

Power off the machine and play out a Hard Reset on the machine.

If this doesn't help, it would be ideal if you contact Member Care through one of the alternatives underneath for further help.

Tangle see demonstrates a dark box

This generally implies the picture chose is unreasonably enormous for the paper or tangle size chose on the machine. You can resolve this through one of the choices underneath:

Diminishing the size of the picture

Increment the paper size

Increment tangle size

Check to ensure the Center Point capacity is killed (utilizing the Center Point include with the beginning situation in the upper left-hand corner will constrain the picture off the edge of the tangle and just demonstrate a dark box on the tangle see.)

Change your Start Position (move it in and down) until you see your picture on the tangle review once more

Check to ensure the Fit to Length capacity is killed. For fit to length, you can likewise change the Mat Size to the 12x24 Landscape Mode tangle or abatement the Fit to Length size.

If that doesn't help, control off the machine and play out a Hard Reset on the machine.

If the Hard Reset doesn't help, if it's not too much trouble contact Member Care through one of the choices underneath for further help.

Cricut Imagine

Stuck on the Welcome (Print. Cut. Envision.) screen

Flips to Menu screen when a picture is chosen

LCD not reacting

Dark box showed on the tangle rather than my chose picture

Faceplate around LCD is tumbling off

Stuck on the Welcome (Print. Cut. Envision.) screen

Contact Member Care through one of the alternatives underneath for further help.

Flips to Menu screen when a picture is chosen

Contact Member Care through one of the alternatives underneath for further help.

LCD not reacting

Power off the machine and play out a Hard Reset on the Imagine machine.

If the Hard Reset doesn't help, it would be ideal if you contact Member Care through one of the choices beneath for further help.

Dim box showed on the tangle rather than my chose picture

When you see a dim box on your tangle in the Project Preview screen, this implies the picture is unreasonably enormous for the paper.

To fix it basically click on the dim box. The picture will show up.

Then snap on the Edit button that resembles a pencil and change the size of your picture so it fits withing the cutting region on the tangle.

Snap "Apply" at the base right of the screen and your picture will show up effectively on the tangle.

Faceplate around LCD is tumbling off

Apply paste or glue to the faceplate of the machine and re-append it to the Imagine machine. This won't harm the machine.

Cricut Gypsy

Flips back to the Welcome screen

Stuck on Loading screen

LCD Unresponsive or Calibration is off

Dark screen - Blue light

LCD split or broken

Flips back to the Welcome screen

Peform a Soft Reset of the Gypsy.

To do this, unscrew the top from the stylus (the part with the circle). On the back of the Gypsy machine, you will see a stick gap above what resembles 3 speaker openings. Stick the pointy end of the stylus top in that pinhole to reset the machine (the Gypsy will simply be fueled OFF). Then power the machine ON and endeavor your venture once more.

If the Soft Reset doesn't help, if it's not too much trouble contact Member Care through one of the alternatives underneath for further help.

Stuck on Loading screen

Peform a Soft Reset of the Gypsy.

To do this, unscrew the top from the stylus (the part with the circle). On the back of the Gypsy machine, you will see a stick opening above what resembles 3 speaker gaps. Stick the pointy end of the stylus top in that pinhole to reset the machine (the Gypsy will simply be controlled OFF). Then power the machine on and endeavor your task once more.

If the Soft Reset doesn't help, it would be ideal if you contact Member Care through one of the alternatives underneath for further help.

LCD Unresponsive or Calibration is off

Endeavor a Hard Reset on the Gypsy.

If Gypsy is ON, control it OFF. Then hold down the upper right silver catch, the silver circle button, and the Power button all simultaneously until a rainbow screen shows up. Then discharge the catches and adhere to the onscreen directions to recalibrate the screen and finish the reset.

If the Hard Reset doesn't help, if you don't mind contact Member Care through one of the alternatives beneath for further help.

Dark screen - Blue light

Endeavor a Hard Reset on the Gypsy.

If Gypsy is ON, control it OFF. Then hold down the upper right silver catch, the silver circle button, and the Power button all simultaneously until a rainbow screen shows up. Then discharge the catches and adhere to the onscreen guidelines to recalibrate the screen and finish the reset. Rehash this procedure twice more. It can take various resets to determine this issue.

If the Hard Reset doesn't resolve the issue, if you don't mind contact Member Care through one of the alternatives beneath for further help.

LCD split or broken

This is an equipment issue.

My Cricut machine is experiencing difficulty understanding cartridges

If you are getting cartridge mistake messages when utilizing your Cricut machine remain solitary, or if the machine isn't perusing the cartridges by any stretch of the imagination, if it's not too much trouble select your machine from the connections underneath and pursue the suggested investigating steps.

Cricut Personal, Cricut Create, Cricut Cake, Cricut Cake Mini, Cricut Expression

Cricut Expression 2

Cricut Imagine

Cricut Personal, Cricut Create, Cricut Cake, Cricut Cake Mini, Cricut Expression

Offer the Cricut a reprieve; turn the Cricut off and enable it to rest for around 10 minutes every hour.

Evacuate the cartridge and set it back in reverse. It is conceivable that the stickers were inappropriately put on the cartridge.

Have a go at utilizing a different cartridge. If the Cricut never again demonstrates the blunder with a different cartridge, contact Member Care through telephone or online talk for help with the cartridge that is provoking the mistake.

Play out a Hard Reset on the machine. If this doesn't help, continue to 5.

If the Cricut keeps on demonstrating the blunder message or demonstrates the mistake message with various cartridges, if you don't mind contact Member Care through one of the alternatives beneath for further help.

Cricut Expression 2

Blunder Message when the cartridge is embedded, Machine doesn't understand cartridges

Expel the cartridge and after that set it back in the Expression 2. If the blunder message comes up, or the machine generally doesn't peruse the cartridge, continue to 2.

Attempt another cartridge in the machine. If this cartridge works, it would be ideal if you contact Member Care for help with the cartridge that isn't working. If the issue happens with all cartridges, it would be ideal if you contact Member Care by means of telephone or online talk for further help.

Cricut Imagine

The machine won't read "heritage" cartridges, or won't perceive Imagine cartridges

"Update Machine" message when embeddings cartridges

The machine won't read "heritage" cartridges, or won't perceive Imagine Cartridges

Attempt another cartridge in the machine. If the subsequent cartridge works in the machine, contact Member Care through one of the alternatives beneath for help with the first cartridge that wasn't working. If the subsequent cartridge likewise doesn't work, it would be ideal if you contact Member Care through one of the alternatives underneath for help.

"Update Machine" message when embeddings cartridges

PRACTICAL EXAMPLES AND STRATEGIES FOR EVERY KIND OF PROJECT

What appeared to be so natural for reasons unknown never was. I never at any point got into entangled undertakings like print and cut, I extremely simply needed to cut vinyl, and for reasons unknown, it just never worked right the first run through. That electronic slicing machine went to a companion or a relative, never to be utilized again.

Then I evaluated the Cricut Explore Air. Furthermore, before I go any further, let me reveal to you how to say Cricut because as a novice to the specialty business, I actually called it Cri-Cut (like cry-cut) everlastingly feeling that it was some extravagant name that solitary use crafters realized how to articulate. It's most certainly not. You articulate it like cricket, the bug.

What's more, if you're somewhat more attentive than I was, you'll see there's charming little cricket recieving wires in the logo. I'm going to credit my idiocy to being pregnant and baby blues mind haze.

CRICUT PROJECTS TO MAKE WITH THE CRICUT MACHINE

Just in the event that you're as terrified of utilizing an electronic cutting machine as I seemed to be, let me give you a little taste of what you can make with it. These tasks are, for the most part, totally different, and all made with the Cricut Explore Air. What's more, I can hardly wait to attempt every one of them!

Here are only a couple of different sorts of things you can do! I likewise incorporated some model Cricut ventures you can make with the Cricut Explore Air from a portion of my preferred shrewd companions!

#1 – CUT PAPER PRODUCTS WITH THE CRICUT EXPLORE AIR

You can go as straightforward or as mind boggling as you need – simply take a gander at this perplexing design from my companion Cori at Hey, Let's Make Stuff!

You can either design your own thing in Cricut Design Space, use designs as of now there, or simply use designs officially made for you in Cricut Design Space!

Sewing Star Pallet Sign

DIY Lunch Notes by Jen Goode

Cut Letter with your Cricut Explore

Straightforward Ice Cream Cone Shirt

The most effective method to Cut Chipboard and wood with the Cricut Explore

Gold Foil Vinyl Wood Teepee

The most effective method to utilize Cricut Design Space on your Ipad and Phone

Utilizing the Cricut Design Space App is an incredible method to make the most of your machine, you can your entrance your pictures, prepared to cut undertakings, and the best part is that you DON'T require web!

If you are as of now acquainted with the Desktop adaptation of Cricut Design Space, you will discover this application exceptionally simple to explore. Simply make a plunge, tap, investigate, and don't be apprehensive, your Phone or Ipad won't detonate!

Then again, if you have no experience at all, this is the best spot for you to be, this book will take you on each and every little symbol the App has.

I comprehend that learning another aptitude can be a bit of baffling at the occasions, however when you take the time and are tolerance with it, you can turn into a specialist.

Since the vast majority of the screen captures you will see next are taken from my iPad, I need to bring up the differences you will discover between the Ipad and Iphone adaptation.

Is there any difference between Design Space App for iPhone and iPad?

Fortunate for you and me there's not by any stretch of the imagination a major difference between these two choices. Would you be able to envision attempting to learn two different applications?

The main little difference between the application for Iphone and Ipad is the SPACE MANAGEMENT.

You will see this first on the top board where it deal (Home – Canvas – Make) on the iPad you will consistently observe the names, yet on the telephone, now and again, you will see a square shape isolated in three equivalent amounts of. Be that as it may, the two of them speak to something very similar.

Something to remember too is that the vast majority of the occasions when you tap on something the menus are long, so with the telephone you should slide them to one side and appropriate to see every one of the choices – now and then with the iPad as well.

Additionally, since space is so restricted, on your telephone the layers catch will be deactivated different the occasions when you tap on different highlights. On the iPad you can leave the layers catch noticeable at unsurpassed.

Understanding the Methodology of this instructional exercise

I think the most ideal approach to learn is by tracking with the way so proceed and – in the wake of getting some espresso/or tea obviously – and open your application from your iPhone or Ipad.

Each time you open your application just because you will be in the home area, from here you will almost certainly pick a prepared to cut venture, pictures and additionally Create a New Project.

When you tap on New Project – the blue square – you will be on the CANVAS AREA. This is where we are going to put the greater part of our endeavors to learn.

I accept that the most ideal approach to learn and ace Cricut Design Space is from the earliest starting point! When you have a reasonable idea of what each symbol and board is for, then you can genuinely dive in and begin investigating further and further.

Here and there we rush to hop from task to extend – Hey That's alright as well! BTDT – But I believe that knowing your work zone will assist you with taking your inventiveness in an unheard of level.

To make this simple for you I have separated the design region in three different segments. Top Panel (purple) Canvas Area (green/Bottom Panel (pink)

Is it true that you are prepared to handle each board/segment and see what happens when you tap any of the choices accessible?

Top Panel

This board enables you to explore from the Canvas to your profile, ventures, and it likewise enables you to extend the Canvas Space to the maximum.

a. Profile Picture – Settings

When you tap on your profile picture, a menu will slide open with two or three settings. From here you can set up your machine and furthermore observe a little application diagram of how the machine functions.

If you are anticipating utilizing Print then Cut choice with your Phone or iPad, this alignment guarantee will that everything will go easily.

There are different alternatives here that I prescribe you to see, I won't broadly expound on them because I wan to concentrate on the designs part of the application.

b. Spare

This alternative will actuate after you've set one component on your canvas region.

I suggest you spare your venture as you go, because, regardless of whether you are working from your gadget and the cloud you can run out battery, your application can crash and if that occurs, there goes your diligent work with it!

c. Home/Canvas/Make

These catches are a type of short code and they speak to the different perspectives you will have while utilizing the application. The darker region speaks to your present area.

Home will take you directly toward the start. If you needed to supplant your present undertaking and include another one tap here.

Canvas: is where you design and sort out a task before you cut it.

Make: tap here if you need to cut your undertaking. First you have to Tap make it on the Bottom Panel.

d. Extend

There are minutes, particularly when you are dealing with a little gadget, that you will need to see your design with ZERO diversions.

When you tap on this choice the Canvas Area will grow and every single other menu will be covered up. To return to your ordinary view, tap here.

Canvas Area

The Canvas region is the place the majority of the enchantment occurs!

This is the place you play with your designs, get innovative, and finish things up before you cut them.

a. Estimations

The canvas region is separated by a lattice!

I think this element is extraordinary, because each and every square you see on the Grid encourages you to envision the cutting mat.

You can change the estimations from creeps to cm and turn the lattice on and off when you tap on the settings symbol situated on the base board of the application.

b. Determination

Whenever you select at least one layers, the determination is blue in shading and you can modify your choice from the majority of the 4 corners.

The red x, is for erasing the layers. The correct upper corner will enable you to pivot the picture. In spite of the fact that if you need a specific edge I prescribe you to utilize the pivot instrument situated in the base board when tapping the symbol Edit.

The little lock keeps the size corresponding when you increment or abatement the size of your layer with the lower right catch of the choice. By tapping on it, you are presently ready to have different extents.

There's additionally a fifth alternative between the lock and the size choice. When you tap on it and drag your design you can see it from different edges. I think this is valuable if you need to find in a 3D point of view (Specially if you have the camera choice initiated). When you let go, the determination will return to its unique structure

Savvy – Hand Gestures

Since we are working with innovation obviously we will be utilizing our fingers a great deal.

It's an extraordinary thought for you to see everything you can do with the tip of your fingers!

There are six signals you can use inside the application:

Tap: utilize a solitary tap to choose a picture or layer (likewise to choose any menu choices)

Swipe: if you have to choose more than one picture, simply swipe your finger on your screen to choose every one of the ones you need.

Tap and hold: You can choose a picture individually also. Complete an increasingly drawn out tap and after that select another design by doing likewise. To expel the determination, simply complete a solitary tap on the canvas territory.

Two Finger swipe: if you have to move around the canvas, you have to utilize 2 fingers simultaneously. Other shrewd you would do motion #2 (Swipe)

Twofold Tap: twofold tap to auto-zoom and see the majority of the components and designs you have on the canvas zone.

Squeeze Zoom: zoom in and out by utilizing your thumb and forefinger.

Base Panel

You folks.... .We are entering profound waters now, and there is no returning!

The base board may feel to you like be the most testing one because basically everything is done from here.

On the Cricut Design Space Desktop form the majority of the choices are isolated in three boards; yet on the application, they are for the most part hanging out together at base, while you become accustomed to it you may get disappointed attempting to discover the choice you need.

Each time you tap on one of the choices; the symbol itself will turn green and the alternatives of that instrument will either take you to another window or will slide open in a white menu simply like I show you on the screen capture directly above.

Note: contingent upon the size of your gadget, with the goal for you to see the majority of the choices of the menu, you should look over every menu to one side and right.

You can just utilize one choice at the time, aside from with the Layers choice, This one can be dynamic consistently. In any case, when the application on you iPhone, the layers board will move toward becoming deactivated all the time.

This application is extremely strong, and It has the greater part of the things that the Desktop form has. Toward the finish of this post, there is a rundown of the things that this application doesn't have.

a. Include Image

Pictures are immaculate when you are assembling your very own undertakings; with them, you can include an additional touch and character to your artworks.

You can look by catchphrase, classes, or cartridges. You can discover pictures you have recently transferred to your PC or your gadget.

Cartridges are a lot of pictures that you have to buy independently. Some of them accompany Cricut Access, and some not. The ones that are not accessible for Cricut Access are authorized brands, for example, Disney, Sesame Street, Hello Kitty, and so on.

Cricut has FREE pictures to cut each week. You can discover them when you tap on Categories.

If you will be looking an activities in the cloud the you would require web; however if you are simply going to utilize pictures you have on your gadget, or apparatuses from the application itself you can work with no web association.

Cool Right?

b. Include Text

Whenever you need to type on the Canvas Area, you should tap on Text.

After you tap you will be incited to pick the textual style you need to work with, and then a little box will show up on the canvas zone for you to type in your content.

c. Include Shapes

Having the option to utilize shapes, it's significant! With them, you can make straightforward, less perplexing, yet at the same time beautiful tasks.

There're are 9 shapes you can look over:

Square

Triangle

Pentagon

Hexagon

Star

Octagon

Heart

The principal alternative isn't a shape, however an astounding and useful asset called Score Line. With this alternative, you can make overlap and score your materials.

If you need to make boxes or love everything about card making, the Score Line will be your closest companion!

d. Transfer

With this alternative, you can transfer your very own records, and pictures that you need to cut. When you Tap on this choice, you will have the choice to pick the area of your photograph, or even take one.

The web is load up with them, and there are huge amounts of bloggers that make extends for nothing. Truth be told I am one of them

If you have no clue where to discover pictures or cut documents, I have a developing library that you can approach when you buy in to my bulletin and become a daydreamer!

e. Activities

The activities boards is a substantial one! From here you can absolutely change your design into a totally different one.

A portion of the choices here might befuddle you from the start, yet as I generally state; don't thump it until you've attempted it!

Gathering – Ungroup

Gathering: tap here to gathering layers. This setting is valuable when you have different layers that make up a perplexing design.

Suppose you are chipping away at an elephant. In all likelihood – and if this is a SVG or cut document – the elephant will be made out of different layers (the body, eyes, legs, trunk, and so forth). If you need to fuse, additional shapes, and content; no doubt is that you will move your elephant over the canvas region a great deal.

By gathering the majority of the elephant layers, you can ensure that everything will remain sort out and nothing will escape place when you move them around then canvas.

Ungroup: This choice will ungroup any assembled layers you select on the canvas region or layers board. This is valuable when you have to alter – size, kind of textual style, and so on – a specific component or layer from the gathering.

Join – Detach

This works like gathering layers; however it's all the more dominant.

When you select the two shapes and tap on append, the two layers will have now a similar shading – shading is dictated by the layer that is on the back – This connection will stay set up, even after I send my task to be cut.

If you want to separate your layers, select them again and tap on, withdraw

Weld

The welding instrument enables you to join to shapes in one.

When I chose the two shapes and tapped on weld, you can see that I made an entirely different shape. The shading is controlled by the layer that is on the back, that is the reason the new shape is pink in shading

Cut

The cut instrument is impeccable to remove shapes, content, and different components, from another designs.

When I chose the two shapes and tapped on cut. You can see that the first record got all cut up. To demonstrate to you what the last item was, I reordered the cut outcome and the isolated the majority of the pieces that came about because of cutting.

Level – Unflatten

This layer is an additional help for the Print and Cut layer characteristic.

When you change the credit from slice to print, that applies to only one layer. Yet, imagine a scenario in which you simply need to do it to numerous shapes at the time.

When you are finished with your designed (you can just unflatten or turn around before leaving your undertaking), select the layers you need to print together all in all, and afterward, tap on level.

On this case, the component was changed over to print and cut. That is the reason it's not demonstrating a dark edge – where the cutting edge will experience – any longer.

Copy

This choice will copy any layers or designs you have chosen on the layers board or canvas region.

This is exceptionally valuable because you don't need to reproduce the design, starting with no outside help. It resembles duplicating and glue.

Shroud Contour

For this model, I consolidated the first design fit as a fiddle with the weld device. Then I composed the word form and cut it against the new shape.

The Contour apparatus enables you to shroud undesirable bits of a design, and it may be initiated when a shape or design has components that can be forgotten about.

When you tap on form, another window will spring up with the majority of the pieces on the design that can be cut of on the left.

For this specific realistic, I concealed the inward circles of the two letters O and the internal piece of the letter R.

Detach Letters

This alternative is accessible for content layers. Fundamentally when you select content and tap on Isolate Layers, you will probably alter each and every letter without anyone else.

The work area form has further developed choices for content, yet this a decent begin. Possibly one they will include different choices.

f. Alter Menu

The alter menu enables you to modify your content significantly further. You can likewise adjust, mastermind, and sort out the majority of the component you have on the canvas territory.

We should see all off the things you can achieve when you tap on this menu.

When you tap on this catch, you can choose any text style you need to use for your undertakings. You can channel them and quest for them on the highest point of window.

If you have Cricut Access, you can utilize any of the considerable number of text styles that have somewhat green A toward the start of the textual style title.

When you pick your text style, you have the alternatives to change its style.

These are the most widely recognized alternatives:

– Regular: This is the default setting. What's more, it wont change the presence of your textual style

– Bold: It will make the text style thicker .

– Italic: It will tilt the textual style to one side.

– Bold italic: it will make the textual style thicker and tilt to one side.

In some cases, the textual style itself will have pretty much choices, The one I utilized for this Screenshot had far more alternatives.

Tip: If you are utilizing Cricut text styles, you will see that with some of them, you can likewise utilize the compose choice.

Arrangement

This arrangement is selective for content. It's incredible for you to compose passages and lines of content.

These are the alternatives you have:

– Left: Align a passage to one side

– Center: Align a passage to the inside

– Right: Align a passage to one side.

Size, Letter, and Line Space

I can't express enough how AMAZING these choices are. Uncommonly the letter separating.

Text dimension: You can transform it physically from here. I regularly simply alter the size of my textual styles from the canvas region.

Letter Space: There are text styles that have a major hole between each letter. This alternative will enable you to diminish the space between letters in all respects effectively. It's genuinely a distinct advantage.

Line Space: this alternative will handle the space between lines in a section. This is valuable because now and then I am compelled to make a solitary lines of content because I am not content with the dividing between lines.

Size

All that you make or type on the Cricut Design Space canvas has a size. You can modify the size from the component in self (when you tap on it). Be that as it may, if you need a component to be an accurate estimation, this choice will enable you to do as such.

Something significant is the little lock on that estimation. When you increment or lessen the size of a picture, the extents are constantly bolted. By tapping on the little lock, you are telling the application that you would prefer not to keep similar extents.

Turn

Much the same as size, pivoting a component is something you can do in all respects effectively from the canvas region. Notwithstanding, there are designs that should be pivoted on a specific point. If that is the situation for you, I really prescribe you to utilize this capacity. Else, you will invest so much energy battling to get a component calculated the manner in which you need it to be.

Flip

If you have to mirror any of your designs on the Cricut Design Space, this is an incredible method to do it.

There are 2 alternatives:

– Flip Horizontal: This will mirror your picture or design on a level plane. Similar to a mirror; It's valuable when you are attempting to make left and right designs. Model: You are making a few wings, or simply have the left wing. With this, you can reorder that equivalent wing and the flip it. Presently you have both!

– Flip Vertical: This is will flip your designs vertically. Sort of like you would see your appearance on water. If you need to make a shadow impact, this choice would be extraordinary for you.

Position

This case demonstrates to you where your components are on the canvas region when you tap on a specific design.

You can move your components around by specifying where you need that component to be situated on the canvas zones. It's exceptionally valuable; however an it's a further developed instrument.

I, for one, don't utilize it that much. I can show signs of improvement with the arrangement devices I am going to make reference to.

Mastermind

Something truly cut about this capacity is that the program will recognize what component is on the front or back and, and when you select it, Design space will actuate the accessible choices for that specific component. Cool right?

These are the choices you get:

– Send to back: This will move the chose component right to the back.

– Move Backward: This alternative will move chosen the component only one stage back. S.o if you have a three component design. It will resemble the cheddar in a cheddar sandwich.

– Move Forward: This choice will move the component only one stage forward. Ordinarily, you would utilize this choice when you have at least 4 components you have to sort out.

– Sent to front: This choice will move the chose component right to the front.

Arrangement

This capacity enables you to adjust the majority of your designs, and it's enacted when select at least 2 components.

– Center: This choices is an exceptionally cool one. When you tap on focus, you are focusing, both vertically and on a level plane; one design against another. This is exceptionally valuable when you need to focus content with a shape like a square or star.

– Align Left: When utilizing this setting, the majority of your components will be adjusted to one side. The uttermost component to one side will direct where the majority of different components will move.

– Align Center: This choice will adjust your components evenly. This will totally focus content and pictures.

– Align Right: When utilizing this setting, the majority of your components will be adjusted to one side. The farthest component to the correct will manage where the majority of different components will move.

– Align Top: This choice will adjust the majority of your chose designs to the top. The uttermost component to the top will direct where the majority of different components will move.

– Align Middle: This alternative will adjust your components vertically. It's valuable when you are working with sections , nd you need them sorted out and adjusted.

– Align Bottom: This alternative will adjust the majority of your chose designs to the base. The uttermost component to the base will direct where the majority of different components will move.

If you need a similar separating between components, it's very tedious to do everything all alone, and it's not 100% right. The appropriate catch will enable you to out with that. For it to be initiated, you should have in any event three components chose.

– Distribute Horizontally: This catch will disperse the components evenly. The uttermost left and right designs will decide the length of the dissemination. This implies the components that are in the inside will be dispersed between the uttermost left and right designs.

ALL YOU NEED TO KNOW TO BECOME A PROFESSIONAL

Did you get a Cricut as of late? If you've ended up considering how to utilize a Cricut, which tangle to utilize and how to finish your first task, this post is for you!

I'll walk you through everything from opening your container, and buying the correct supplies to finishing your absolute first task!

Would it be a good idea for me to Buy A Cricut Maker?

All things considered, first of all... here's a little foundation on the Cricut Maker. The Cricut Maker is an electronic cutting machine (additionally called an art plotter or bite the dust cutting machine). You can consider it like a printer; you make a picture or design on your PC, cell phone, or tablet, and after that send it to the machine. Then again, actually as opposed to printing your design, the Maker removes it of whatever material you need! (The Maker can cut more than 100 different materials! Here's a rundown of 100+ materials that a Cricut Maker can cut.)

The Cricut Maker is extraordinary for crafters, quilters, sewers, DIYers, and any other person with an inventive streak! It has a versatile apparatus framework that enables you to switch among cutting edges and extras so you can do any sort of task. Need to cut sewing examples and texture? Change to the revolving cutting edge. Need to cut balsa wood or calfskin? Change to the knife cutting edge. Need to draw something, or add scoring lines to your undertaking? The Cricut pen and scoring wheel are immaculate! Regardless of what kind of undertaking you need to do, the Cricut Maker can deal with it!

What's more, to demonstrate you exactly that it is so natural to make amazing things with a Cricut Maker, I have a too straightforward cowhide bow venture instructional exercise toward the finish of this post. It'll take you under 10 minutes! I additionally made a fast video that strolls you through the whole starting arrangement your Maker machine, including making your first venture: an adorable welcome card. Look at it to see exactly that it is so natural to utilize the machine!

Will I utilize the machine enough to justify the cost?

This is the issue I hear regularly, and it's absolutely reasonable! The Cricut Maker is typically $399.99 (however you can generally discover it at a bargain), which is surely a speculation. Nobody needs to spend that sort of money on something that will get utilized each day for a month and afterward simply lounge around social occasion dust!

However, I wouldn't stress over that with the Cricut Maker; there are SO MANY different things you can do with it. I don't think you'll ever get exhausted. I've had my Cricut machines throughout recent years despite everything I use them consistently! If you're searching for task thoughts, I have a Pinterest board loaded up with Cricut ventures, and here's a rundown of more than 100 art and DIY ventures you can make with a Cricut machine.

What additional items do I have to utilize the machine, and how costly will it be?

The Cricut Maker accompanies completely all that you have to utilize the machine directly in the container! It even has test materials so you can make your absolute first venture immediately!

All things considered, probably the coolest thing about the Maker is that is has a versatile instrument framework which enables you to change out the sharp edges and devices to do different kinds of activities. The Maker accompanies a fine-point sharp edge (the standard edge for everything from paper to card stock), a fine-point pen for illustration, and a rotational edge for cutting texture. It likewise accompanies a LightGrip tangle (for paper and so forth.) and a FabricGrip tangle for cutting texture with the rotational sharp edge. Between those two cutting edges and those two mats, you can cut pretty much anything you need. You could utilize your Maker each and every day with simply the things that come in the container for always, and you'd never get exhausted!

Obviously, there are extras and additional items you can purchase for your machine if you need. Cricut is continually turning out with new apparatuses and sharp edges; however the most well-known additional items for a Maker are:

The knife edge (about $45, except if you discover it at a bargain): enables you to cut thicker materials like balsa wood or calfskin

The scoring wheels (about $40, except if you discover them on special): permits you make fresh, clean score lines in your activities

Extra pens or markers (about $12 for a 5-pack, except if you discover them at a bargain): comes in huge amounts of hues and thicknesses, including metallics, sparkles, fine point, and calligraphy pens

The other spot you could spend extra cash if you need to is in the Cricut picture and text styles library. It is allowed to utilize Cricut Design Space (their online design programming), and they have huge amounts of pictures and textual styles that you can use for nothing. What's more, obviously, you can generally transfer your very own pictures and utilize those.

If you would prefer not to utilize your very own pictures, the library has more than 50,000 pictures, several text styles, huge amounts of prepared to-make ventures, authorized characters, and so on that you can use for your tasks. What's more, extremely, a LOT of it is free! In any case, for certain things, you need to buy the picture or text styles before you can utilize them in your activities. You can purchase pictures exclusively (normally about $0.99) or in cartridges or "sets" (more often than not about $5 to $30), and once you've gotten them you can utilize them in a boundless number of tasks.

You can likewise pursue Cricut Access, which is their month to month membership which gives you access to more than 50,000 pictures and 400 textual styles, in addition to a 10% markdown on some other Cricut items! Cricut Access memberships are $7.99/month or $9.99/month for their Premium enrollment, which gives you free delivering and up to half off authorized text styles, pictures, and prepared to-make extends (the authorized stuff like Disney characters and so on is excluded in the 50,000 free pictures because, well, it's authorized!)

What materials would i be able to cut?

Pretty much anything you need! The Cricut Maker can slice materials up to 2.4mm thick, and it can cut stuff as slight and fragile as tissue paper. Here's a rundown of 100+ materials that a Cricut Maker can cut.

What sorts of texture would i be able to cut, and do I need a supporter?

Indeed, I simply shared a rundown of 100+ materials a Cricut can cut; however, texture is somewhat exceptional and gets its own different segment!

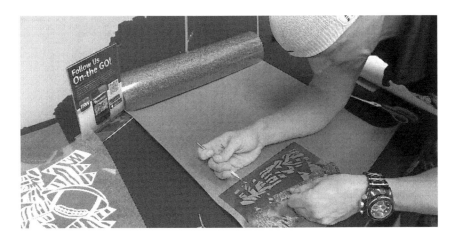

Perhaps the coolest thing about the Maker is that it enables you to cut texture without a supporter when you utilize the turning edge! Past adaptations of the Cricut machines had the option to cut texture with the normal fine-point edge; however you needed to stiffen it up first by putting interfacing on the back of the texture. That is fine and all, yet now and again you don't need interfacing on the back of your task, which is the reason the revolving sharp edge is great. (Furthermore, the fine-point sharp edge is positively ready to cut texture;

however the edges of the cuts aren't really excessively perfect and fresh... the revolving cutting edge completes a MUCH better activity!)

The Maker can cut practically any texture, from sensitive textures like tulle and ribbon to substantial textures like denim, sailcloth, and burlap. It can likewise cut "claim to fame" textures like sequined textures, texture with sparkle on it, calfskin, fake hide, and even blanket batting. When you utilize the rotating cutting edge to cut texture, you needn't bother with a supporter; you can put the texture straightforwardly onto the FabricGrip tangle and cut it without anyone else. Or on the other hand, if you need a support on your texture, don't hesitate to connect the sponsorship before you cut; the turning edge can deal with the two layers with no issue! Truth be told, the Maker can slice up to three layers of texture simultaneously, which is magnificent for things like blanket making or texture ventures with numerous pieces in a similar shape.

Will it be simple for me to get familiar with the product and use it to design my own venture or prepare to-make ventures?

That's right, I suspect as much! I really imagine that Cricut Design Space is quite natural, regardless of whether you're not by any means well informed. Cricut has a little walkthrough instructional exercise that you experience when you initially set up your machine, and it completes a truly great job of demonstrating to you the nuts and bolts of Design Space (in any event, enough to make any of the prepared to-make extends in the Cricut library). Also, if you need to design your very own ventures, I have a lot of well ordered instructional exercises on the most proficient method to utilize a Cricutthat you can look at.

If you're still somewhat apprehensive, I made a video that strolls you through the whole introductory arrangement of your Cricut Maker, including making your absolute first undertaking! It tells you the best way to utilize the fundamental elements of Design Space to make a basic welcome card.

What sorts of specialties and DIY undertakings would i be able to make?

As far as possible, here is your creative mind! You can make basically anything from welcome cards and paper ventures to home stylistic theme to wedding/party/occasion enrichments to attire and blankets. There are such a large number of different things you can make that I'd always be unable to show them all. Be that as it may, here is a rundown of 100+ specialties and DIY ventures you can make with a Cricut, and here is my Pinterest board brimming with Cricut venture thoughts; those will at any rate kick you off!

Would i be able to utilize my old cartridges?

The first Cricut machines utilized physical plastic cartridges that you could embed into the machine itself to access picture content. The physical cartridges have been resigned, and now Cricut has computerized cartridges (essentially a "picture set" of related pictures accessible in the Cricut library).

Be that as it may, don't stress! If you have physical cartridges from a past Cricut machine, you can absolutely still utilize those pictures! You can connect your physical cartridge to the advanced form in Cricut Design Space, and afterward, you can utilize the computerized variant of the majority of your pictures whenever you need.

Would i be able to transfer my very own pictures?

That's right! Here is a well ordered instructional exercise telling you the best way to transfer your very own pictures to Cricut Design Space. You can transfer fundamental pictures like a jpeg or png, or you can transfer a vector record if you have a picture that has numerous layers. Design Space supports transfer of the accompanying document types:

jpg

gif

png

bmp

svg

dxf

If you have questions that weren't replied in this post, don't hesitate to email me and ask them! I'm constantly glad to help!

As guaranteed, here is a fast instructional exercise on making calfskin bows with a Cricut Maker. This undertaking requires a Cricut Maker, the knife cutting edge, a StrongGrip tangle, and a bit of calfskin.

Begin by opening up this calfskin bow venture in Cricut Design Space. If you click the green Make It catch, the bow is now measured to be 1″ tall and about 2.5″ wide. If you need to change the size or make various duplicates, click the Customize catch to open the undertaking in Design Space.

Select "Book of clothing Leather" in the materials segment, and the product will instruct you to stack the knife edge in your Maker. Open Clamp B, expel the fine-point sharp edge and introduce the knife edge, so the apparatuses on the cutting edge meet with the riggings in the machine. Close the clasp.

Spot your calfskin on the StrongGrip tangle, face up, then burden the tangle into the machine. Press the glimmering Go catch, and the machine will begin to cut! (If this is the first occasion when you've utilized your knife cutting edge, the product will walk you through adjusting the knife sharp edge, so you get exact cuts.)

After the machine gets done with writing, it will request that you check the slice to ensure it's gone right through the material. Ensure you don't empty the tangle first! Simply twist the tangle somewhat directly at the edge of a cut, and if you can see right through the material to the tangle underneath, then you're ready. If it didn't carve entirely through, press the Go catch again to make it cut once again.

What Comes with the Cricut Maker?

Cricut Maker with Fine Point Blade

We should Get Started Box (Included URL for arrangement)

Welcome Book and Rotary Blade

Fine Point Pen

Guarantee

USB Cord and Power Cord

A Piece of Cardstock and Fabric (for your first task)

12 x 12 Light Grip and Fabric Grip Mat

50 Free Ready-to-Make Projects, Including 25 Sewing Patterns

Free Trial Membership to Cricut Access™ (for new endorsers)

Which Cricut Mat Should I Use?

Blue Light Grip Mat

This tangle is perfect for light weight materials. It gives enough hold to keep the material set up during slicing yet enables it to be effectively evacuated without tearing.

Printer Paper, Vellum, Light Cardstock, Construction Paper, Vinyl and Cardstock

Green Standard Mat

The standard tangle is perfect for the amplest assortment of materials. It gives a more grounded grasp which enables it to immovably hold heavier materials set up with simple.

Designed Paper, Vinyl, Iron-On, Cardstock, Embossed Cardstock, Heavey Cardstock

Purple Strong Grip Mat

The most grounded of the Cricut mats, this tangle is ideal for thick and heavyweight materials. It highlights twofold life glue innovation, which enables it to effectively grasp onto increasingly strong materials and hold them set up all through the cutting procedure.

Forte Cardstock, Chipboard, Backed Fabrics, Leather, Magnet Sheet, and Felt

Pink Fabric Mat

The texture tangle is produced using higher-quality PVC to withstand expanded cutting weight. It includes a different glue than the other cutting mats settling on it the perfect decision for texture and th ideal counterpart for the Cricut Rotary Blade.

Silk, Canvas, Burlap, Cotton, and that's only the tip of the iceberg

The most effective method to Use A Cricut Mat

To utilize the glue Cricut cutting mat, expel the unmistakable defensive liner. Spot it to the side while the tangle is being used and place it back on the tangle once you have completed the process of utilizing it.

Spot the material you are working with (right side up) inside the 12" x 12" matrix, ensuring that the whole material has clung to the tangle completley.

Which Cricut Accessories Do I Need To Get Started Crafting?

I suggest obtaining an Essential Tool Set before you start creating! This will have the majority of the things you have to make stunning tasks rapidly and effectively!

This instrument set incorporates:

Invert Tweezers to lift and verify sensitive materials

Weeder enables you to expel little negative pieces from the design

Scissors with Protective Cover

Calculated Spatula to lift materials from the tangle without bowing them

Scrubber to polish materials and clean cutting mats

Scoring Stylus to make crease lines on cards

12″ Wide Material Trimmer to precisely cut Vinyl, Iron-On, and Cardstock

Swap Blades for Trimmer

Scoring Blade for Trimmer to add scoring lines to different tasks

What Supplies Should I Purchase?

I prescribe obtaining a wide range of materials so you can get familiar with the wide assortment of materials that your Cricut Maker is equipped for cutting. The following are a couple of the materials I would prescribe acquiring!

Removable Vinyl Variety Pack 12 x 12

Move Tape

Ordinary Iron-On Rainbow Sampler

Cardstock Rainbow Sampler 12 x 24

Texture Sampler Pack

Felt Sampler Pack

5 Pen Variety Pack

Knife Blade

Scoring Wheels

What's the Difference among Vinyl and Iron-On?

There are two different kinds of Vinyl, Adhesive vinyl which has a sticky support and is connected with weight and Iron-On (additionally alluded to as Heat Transfer Vinyl) which has a paste backing that is actuated by warmth.

Iron-On and Heat Transfer Vinyl

Iron-On is perfect for ventures that can withstand heat. The surface ought to be smooth and ready to have an iron connected to it. Instances of appropriate materials are:

Shirts

Texture

Cushions

Wood

Cardstock

Canvas Tote Bags

Iron-On has a paste backing that clings to a surface once it's been initiated by warmed. YOu can apply Iron-On with an iron, EasyPress or Heat Press. You can peruse progressively about the Easy Press here.

A reasonable defensive liner is situated over the Iron-On, this enables the vinyl to be warmed without being harmed and is stripped far from the design once it has clung to the material. Iron-On should be cut with the liner side (really side) confronting downwards and any content or pictures ought to be turned around or reflected.

Glue Vinyl

Vinyl is perfect for surfaces that are hard just as smooth. Instances of things that can have vinyl concerned them are mugs, wood, dividers, mirrors, and glass. It tends to be cut with the correct side confronting upwards and the liner confronting downwards towards the Cricut tangle.

How Do I Clean My Cricut Mats and Fabric Mat?

To clean the Cricut Light, Standard and Strong Grip Mats absorb the tangle warm foamy water. Delicately perfect any remaining buildup with Non-Alcohol Baby Wipes. Utilize your Scraper to expel any difficult bits of buildup.

To clean the pink Cricut Fabric Grip tangle basically expel any stray strings with a lot of invert tweezers. The glue is different on this tangle and ought not be washed!

HOW TO TURN YOUR CREATIVITY INTO AN AMAZING BUSINESS

Neighborhood deals can be separated into two sections, business to business (B2B) and business to client (B2C). If you choose to be a neighborhood merchant, it's ideal to pick between one of these two fragments.

These two gatherings don't have much cover in the things they buy, or where you can market to them. The reasonable entrepreneur won't squander their time pursuing leads and tossing showcasing cash at customers they aren't arrangement to help.

Business to Business –

Volume Sales - The objective here is to utilize the productivity of creating in bigger numbers to drive the cost you pay per thing down. The bigger the generation run, the lower your expense for item and time per unit created. This is the hardest work to get into for another Cricut or Silhouette based business. The open doors are less, and the customer desires are higher.

Models:

An agreement with the neighborhood government or school to deliver shirts or signage.

Yearly occasion signage and promoting, for example, signage and shirts for the Susan G. Komen Foundation

Aces –

Regularly, legally binding work can be finished in a solitary session. This implies you can buy from sellers in mass, enabling you to arrange lower material expenses. You will likewise have less exchanging between vinyl hues or product offerings, which means you can accomplish more in less time. This leaves you with more opportunity for different undertakings or showcasing endeavors.

Cons –

It will be hard to get one of these agreements. As a matter of fact, I haven't attempted. It is sensible to expect that these open doors in your locale are now being served by another person. If they aren't, jump at the opportunity.

Custom Work – Custom work for business clients, can be an incredible gig with enormous upside. Organizations are happy to pay as much as possible for quality, solid work. You can work with organizations to help make a brand character, make mindfulness, and make special promotions.

Models:

If a business is simply beginning, you can offer a business dispatch starter pack. At least, you ought to incorporate logo design, signage for a retail front, and establishment.

You can likewise offer organization marked swag like shirts, cups, or mugs as an extra. Every one of these administrations can be independent for new or existing organizations.

Signage, for example, sandwich sheets or yard signs.

Stars –

You are making associations with developing organizations. After your first effective exchange, you become their place of contact for future business marking, decals, mindfulness materials, and even visual depiction. This relationship can pay future profits.

Business customers accompany numerous open doors for up selling. More often than not, it is a success win for both of you.

Cons –

It very well may be difficult to discover new, quality leads. For most existing organizations, they as of now have a sign organization they trust. All things considered, they needed to get their unique signs some place, isn't that so?

Entrepreneurs will, in general, be shrewd, with elevated requirements and a solid feeling of what is a suitable cost for your administration. Try not to be shocked or insulted if they get various offers and arrange cost before tolerating your offer.

Business to Customer–

Volume Sales - These standards are equivalent to with business to business mass work, yet you're going to discover your clients in new places and have different contributions.

You will sell things that retail clients need to purchase. This incorporates one of a kind shirt, tumblers, espresso cups, or whatever else you can think of. The key is to have expansive intrigue, something you can create various with the desire that they will sell.

Models:

Leasing a space at a classical shopping center or art reasonable. Make sure to evaluate how much space you really need, the value per square foot, and the commission your landowner is requesting.

Become a seller at neighborhood occasions. For instance, my wife was a merchant at the Mutt Strut in Nashville, Tennessee this year.

Discover space in popup shops

Discover occasional occasions in your town that offer shabby or free retail space, similar to a rancher's market or occasion reasonable.

Go out business cards to neighborhood shops where you envision your items may sell well.

Aces –

Your imagination will be the driver of your deals. If you concoct a sharp thought with mass or specialty claim, and you are in the opportune spot to offer it, you will receive the benefits. Additionally, you get the opportunity to figure out what media and medium you work in. Shirts, mugs, or whatever else, the decision is yours.

Cons –

You'll require a retail space to offer your things. The spots with higher pedestrian activity will be progressively costly, yet pedestrian activity doesn't really rise to deals.

To be effective, you'll should be eager to explore different avenues regarding different areas and item contributions.

Custom Work –

Models:

One of a kind shirts for a wedding party

Divider decals with one of a kind statements and family names

Monograms for wine glasses or vehicle decals

Experts –

Custom work for nearby clients has the most reduced startup cost of any of these procedures. If you can locate a solid seller who offers materials in little bunches, you can concede putting resources into vinyl until you secure a task.

You can likewise do the majority of your work from home, evading the need to put resources into a retail front or work space.

You will almost certainly charge a premium for your work. Retail clients pay the most astounding costs, and your design customization will raise the cost as well.

Cons –

Once more, leads will be difficult to get. Toward the start, verbal exchange might be the main device you have. You're going to need to concentrate on quality workmanship and reasonable valuing to get your underlying deals. If you have a touch of cash, you can kick begin the procedure by showcasing with a neighborhood Facebook promotion.

Selling Online

Concentrating on web based selling requires a higher specialized learning base, at the same time, as I can verify, you don't need to be a software engineer to make it work. You can profit with vinyl online by giving quality custom work, turning into a data center, or giving mass contributions. Once more, it's not prudent to attempt to do every one of the three.

Your time is best spent working in one of the three choices to start. In this way, if you choose to give custom work, don't likewise attempt to turn into a data center simultaneously. In the wake of building up your underlying balance and getting beneficial deals, you can anticipate how to utilize that cash for developing into different classifications.

Custom Work – This is the manner by which I got my begin. For the correct individual, I really accept this is an incredible method to the opening shot your Silhouette or Cricut vinyl business.

Through existing commercial centers or your own site, you can turn into the one they go to.

Models:

Existing sites that enable you to sell specially craft administrations. Etsy, Amazon Custom, and Amazon Handmade are the most notable. Different choices incorporate Artfire, DaWanda, Bonanza, Depop, and Tictail

Another alternative is to dispatch your very own site. An incredible case of this can be seen with A Great Impression. They propelled a rousing divider decal site, alongside a specially craft administration. You can get any decal, in any size you need from them.

Tip: I would suggest their procedure. Discover a specialty little enough you can contend inside, and offer hand crafts from that point.

Masters -

If you sell on a current stage, the startup expenses are exceptionally low. The minute you dispatch, you're contending in the worldwide marketplace. You approach a large number of potential clients.

Furthermore, one of a kind designs will enable you to charge an excellent rate. Nonetheless, online custom costs will, in general, be lower than a similar work done locally. It's an opportunity to clean up and expand your design range of abilities too.

Cons -

Access to the whole world additionally implies you are going up against anybody with a web association. Expanded challenge will prompt lower costs for your designs and difficulty getting occupations if you aren't intensely valued or offering an extraordinary design viewpoint.

Selling on the web implies you likewise need to learn coordination. You're going to need to get entered in with a transportation organization, make sense of pressing material, and calculate that cost your estimating.

Volume Sales – The advantages of doing work in mass online are equivalent to neighborhood. By accomplishing more work without a moment's delay and diminishing the occasions we make switches between hues, designs, and product offerings, you're driving the expense per unit created down. You'll discover your clients through existing sites or by building up your own.

Models:

The greatest stages for mass design work are eBay and Amazon, in spite of the fact that Etsy has seen development in these sorts of offers in the course of the most recent three years. On these stages, you can sell window decals, moving expressions, divider specks, vehicle decals, shirts, and so on. Essentially, anything with an extreme interest that you can replicate various occasions after the underlying design.

Another alternative is to pick a specialty and offer a similar sort of work without anyone else site. Spotted Decals is an incredible case of this strategy. They are a little organization that works in divider specks just, nothing else. They are the expert when it comes to spotted decals. Because it is specialty and repeatable, the work should be possible in mass, and they face negligible challenge.

Geniuses -

You can begin to manufacture a genuine retail business selling this sort of work. After some time, you will most likely figure out what the interest for the designs you offer and plan generation ahead as needs be. This will build your productivity and lower the

You'll additionally be making more items. In all actuality, you will acquire less cash per deal; however this will allow you to purchase vinyl in mass at a diminished cost.

Cons -

You're going toward the world here. There's a huge amount of rivalry, so the edges will be lower, and quite possibly's somebody can undermine your little edges with phony or fake things anytime.

It's takes significant stage information to sell on the majority of the different commercial centers (eBay, Amazon, Etsy, and so on.).

Data Hub – Have you at any point visited a blog for guidance on the best way to utilize your machine or undertaking motivation? If you can dispatch a site and become the expert in the field, there's a chance to profit with your Silhouette Cameo or Cricut there as well.

Models - There are some extraordinary instances of web journals offering specialized expertise and task motivation with a specialty shaper. Some likewise couple their Cricut and Silhouette learning with a lifestyle blog.

Satisfaction's Life

Only a Girl and Her Blog

Cutting for Business

Ginger Snap Crafts

Lia Griffith

Salty Canary

CutCutCraft

Stars -

You're not making decals for clients any longer, and yourventures pursue your course of events. This implies you get the chance to be particular about the posts you take on, and the time you put into an undertaking. Additionally, you can express your inventiveness anyway you'd like and manufacture the group of spectators you need.

Cons -

How about we repeat, you're not making decals for clients any longer. This plan of action is totally different than the remainder of the choices I've spread out.

You can adapt your site with promotions, supported posts, offering an information item like a book for your devoted perusers, or a physical item. Be that as it may, regardless of which course you take, it's not as immediate, nor basic, as selling a decal.

STEP BY STEP INSTRUCTIONS TO CUT PDF SEWING PATTERNS ON THE CRICUT MAKER

I'm infatuated with my new Cricut Maker! It's fast and simple to change over your PDF examples to be removed on this stunning new machine. Regardless of whether you don't have the Cricut Maker, you can utilize your other Cricut machines (Explore Air, and Explore Air2) to remove your paper example pieces as well! I utilize mine everything an opportunity to make my doll garments sewing quicker and increasingly exact. As a designer of doll garments PDF designs, this machine has made my activity speedier and simpler after a little set up regardless.

I got my Cricut Maker for Christmas. I've been utilizing cricut machines since they originally turned out and have possessed every single one that they have made. I think this Maker machine is a distinct advantage for the doll garments network, particularly if you sew for specialty fairs. I have a feeling that I've been hanging tight for it the majority of my "sewing" life. You would now be able to cut texture by essentially laying it on the tangle. There is no compelling reason to apply any stiffener so as to cut it with this phenomenal, new machine. The Cricut Maker is the main machine that has another rotational cutting sharp edge that was specifically made for texture. See progressively about this astounding machine here!

The Cricut Design Space library has many sewing designs for dolls. They cost about equivalent to the PDF designs you purchase from Oh Sew Kat! However, consider the possibility that don't care for those styles , r you need to make something other than what's expected. I've assembled this essential instructional exercise to walk you through the means of how to cut your Oh Sew Kat! PDF designs on your Cricut Maker machine (or cut your paper designs on other cricut machines-likewise a help!) There are numerous approaches to do this, however ,this is the strategy I have utilized , nd once you do it more than once, it's extremely quite speedy!

If you don't mind NOTE: Sharing a SVG record (on the web or face to face) you make from a PDF Pattern you acquired is equivalent to sharing the example document, and it is illicit. If you have companions that you need to impart to, it would be ideal if you respect the designer's diligent work and direct them to buy their own duplicate The Design Space programming does not peruse PDF documents. You should change over the example piece pages to .SVG documents so as to bring them into Design Space. There are various approaches to do this. Despite the fact that bringing in the example pieces in pages or gatherings may appear to be enticing, I don't suggest it. Over the long haul, it will be simpler to work with your records if you spare each example piece as a different document. (This will give you a chance to orchestrate the pieces on the slicing mat to lessen the texture utilized, and will be certainly justified regardless of the additional exertion in advance.)

I use Adobe Illustrator to change over my documents. There are other realistic projects accessible on the web. You need one that will peruse a PDF record, and furthermore spare as a SVG document. When you open the PDF document in another program, spare it as another record with another name, so you don't lose your unique, printable example and directions. I name it something like "Popsicle Top 18 Cricut Maker" to differentiate it from my printable documents. (There is additionally a site called PICSVG that I use to make SVG documents from jpg and png records. It's an extraordinary asset to give a shot too.

You just need the diagrams of the example pieces and each piece ought to be spared as an individual SVG record. Utilize the "utilization artboard" check box to keep the measuring right. If an example piece should be cut on a crease, you have to copy that piece, and after that flip it, and join the lines to make one piece. You need to ensure the lines are covered only a hair! Line the two up precisely, so you have the full piece (the

Maker will cut a solitary layer of texture there are no folds.) Delete the covering lines and weld the sort out into one shape. Contingent upon how the example piece is arranged on the page, you may need to change or turn a piece or two to get it precisely right. Guarantee each example piece is arranged here and there as per the grain line and you additionally need to ensure they are that way when you cut them.

Open Cricut Design Space and make another task. From the left menu, click UPLOAD. Discover your svg records you made on your PC, and transfer them every individually. When they are altogether stacked, add them to your canvas. They will import in dark. I change the shade of the pieces to enable me to keep them all straight. I utilize a different shading for each size doll, and afterward,, guarantee that the pieces that would be cut from different textures are additionally spared in different hues so they will cut on different mats. (For instance, an example that has a top and jeans would have two hues.) Once you have imported your SVGs, set aside the effort to stack a bit of duplicate paper in your cricut machine. Cut out the pieces and contrast them with your printed PDF duplicate to guarantee they are actually the equivalent.

Copy any pieces you have to cut more than one of. One of those should be reflected if they are not the equivalent. For instance, sleeves generally simply should be copied. A bodice back, be that as it may, should be copied with one reflected, so you have a privilege and left back bodice. Rather than bringing in a belt or lash, I just make a square shape in Design Space, giving it a different shading if important to keep it on a different tangle. Some shorts with a front and a back that are different example pieceswill have four different example pieces in your Design Space record. Spare your record so you can utilize it again later!

IT'S EASY TO CUT FABRIC ON THE CRICUT MAKER TO MAKE DOLL CLOTHES.

Lay your texture on your tangle. I like to utilize this device to smooth it out. There are two different ways you can preserve your texture when cutting doll garments on the Cricut Maker. When you hit MAKE IT, you can without much of a stretch move the pieces around and between the mats, yet make certain to keep the pieces arranged accurately for the grain and for directional prints. You can likewise mastermind the pieces before you hit MAKE IT, on your canvas, then ATTACH them to keep their dividing. If you are utilizing the cricut application, attempt the snap tangle where you can put your example pieces straightforwardly on to your formed or pre-cut pieces!

Cut out your example pieces, and sew your doll garments together as indicated by the guidelines. The biggest cricut tangle is 12×24 inches. You may require more than one tangle to cut the majority of your pieces, and most 18 inch doll skirts won't fit on the tangle by any stretch of the imagination. I typically cut the skirt out while the Maker is taking a shot at different pieces and complete both on the double! Here are two cricut packs that will make your tasks somewhat simpler: Cricut Sewing Kit and the Cricut Brayer and Mat Remover Set.

Top Questions Every Cricut Beginner Wants to Know

It is safe to say that you are attempting to choose if you need to purchase a Cricut or are a Cricut learner and confounded on where to begin? You're in the correct spot because prepare to be blown away. The vast majority (myself included) had precisely the same inquiries when beginning. In this way, don't get disappointed and how about we handle the Cricut Beginner FAQ now:

It sounds straightforward, yet I ensure that you will be astonished at the quantity of ventures you can make in a small amount of the time you would almost certainly do them by hand. I'm talking sewing designs, organizer stickers, wooden signs for your home, monogrammed mugs thus considerably more!

This machine is ideal for the imaginative individual who consistently needs to do DIY extends however is lacking in time,, so they sit on your Pinterest load up rather. Also if you have a hand crafted business or Etsy shop, I can practically promise you will get a huge amount of incentive out of this machine.

2. Would i be able to transfer my very own pictures to use with Cricut?

Indeed! You can transfer your very own pictures or any of our free SVG and Me cut records that are now arranged to be absolutely good with Cricut Design Space.

There are a wide range of picture document types out there. The best kind (that we give) are SVGs, which stands (lemme put on my geeky glasses here) versatile vector realistic. Fundamentally, it utilizes math equations to make the picture dependent on focuses between lines. Try not to stress I can see your eyes staring off into the great unknown and won't go in more profundity than that.

The advantage of this is the SVG designs can be broadened without getting that hazy pixelated look you see with other document types, making them totally wonderful for making undertakings of any size!

If you haven't as of now ensure you look at our Free SVG Library which has huge amounts of designs that you can transfer to Design Space today to get making in minutes.

3. What different materials would i be able to cut with Cricut?

Everybody will, in general, consider Cricut machines as cutting paper or vinyl, yet the fact of the matter is there are a LOT more things that a Cricut can cut. Truth be told, the Cricut Explore Air 2 can cut more than 60 sorts of materials!

For example, it can cut chipboard, balsa (very flimsy) wood, magnet material, aluminum (otherwise known as soft drink jars), thus considerably more! For thicker materials, you will need to move up to the profound cut cutting edge for the best cut quality.

Also, the new Cricut Maker can cut EVEN more materials (100+ actually) with 100x the weight intensity of the Explore Air 2. It's strength you inquire? Texture! It has a fresh out of the box new revolving sharp edge which makes it an unquestionable requirement for sewers that can now prepare an undertaking in minutes rather than hours.

Need to see a full rundown of materials and the cutting settings for each? Look at this.

4. What sorts of DIY ventures would i be able to make with a Cricut?

Truly, maybe the best AND most overpowering piece of purchasing a Cricut is that it is SO flexible that you don't have the foggiest idea where to start. In this way, oppose the data over-burden and attempt to concentrate on one anticipate at once.

The amusing thing about Cricut ventures is that, when I was beginning, I will think about a zillion undertakings or see some on Pinterest and think "hello, I wanna make that!" Then, I plunk down to make a task, and my brain would go absolutely clear!

Indeed, to help with this, I thought of a HUGE rundown of Cricut ventures (that will keep on developing so continue returning for updates). You can peruse through, pick one from the rundown, and get creating in a matter of moments! Also, it presently accompanies a FREE printable adaptation you can allude to for motivation. Along these lines, ensure you head over and download that if you don't have it.

5. Will it be simple for me to figure out how to utilize Cricut Design Space to make my very own custom activities?

That's right, and I'm here to help! Look at our Cricut instructional exercises page here, which a great spot for amateurs to begin! We include new recordings every week and even give accommodating free assets and agendas so ensure you return frequently.

You don't have to claim a Cricut to begin rehearsing with Design Space. When you get your machine, you'll be a stage ahead!

6. What supplies do I have to begin?

This is one of the inquiries I had the hardest time replying as a fledgling. I scanned for a printable asset on the web and was stunned when I couldn't discover one – so I chose to make my own to impart to you!

I took a huge amount of time inquiring about, getting counsel from others, and afterward accumulating this tremendous rundown of Essential Cricut Supplies Every Beginner Should Have that I am offering to you (fortunate duck) to spare all of you the time it took me

It will ceaselessly be refreshed, so ensure you inquire intermittently to ensure you have the most recent rendition. Likewise, let me know if you have any sacred goal Cricut items or tips that I ought to incorporate!

IS BUYING A CRICUT WORTH IT?

I was visiting with a companion a day or two ago who was thinking about purchasing a Cricut Explore. At $299 ($249 at a bargain!), it is anything but an economical buy and she was thinking about whether she'd use it enough to justify the cost. I believe it's a substantial inquiry if you're pondering purchasing a Cricut. So I needed to discuss the reasons that it's an incredible buy — and several reasons you should need to pause.

MOTIVATIONS TO BUY A CRICUT

I've said this a couple of times in different posts, yet when I initially found out about the Cricut I truly thought I had no utilization for such a machine. I thought it was primarily for scrapbookers and since I didn't scrapbook, I never investigated. In any case, seeing it in real life live, getting a

Cricut myself, and working with the Cricut group throughout the most recent three years, I've come to understand this is completely probably the best apparatus I claim for making a wide range of things. These are a couple of my preferred motivations to purchase a Cricut, however there are numerous a lot additionally relying upon your needs!

To begin with, the Cricut Explore is so unimaginably flexible. I realize I make a ton of undertakings here that are specifically for the blog and designed to rouse you to make things all alone. Be that as it may, I am additionally always utilizing it for ventures that never come around here. Just as of late I've made marks for provisions in my art room, craftsmanship for the kid's room, confetti, custom tote sacks and diaries for our ladies' retreat, shirts for a companion's child's first birthday celebration party, improvements for a Bunco party, vinyl names for an infant shower support, shirts for a Firefly-themed party, and a few other arbitrary cut documents for companions. I cherish that I can make such a large number of sorts of tasks with the Cricut and that I can utilize my Cricut and cunning abilities to assist my less-shrewd companions with their activities.

Second, it will spare you so much time. If you're utilized to hand cutting, the Cricut can do it so a lot quicker and better — and it will spare your hands (my hands spasm so gravely with scissors!). I can't accept the amount more I can do because my

Cricut makes making quicker. Our gatherings have a great time components because I can make things quite a lot more rapidly than designing and cutting by hand. Furthermore, I get the opportunity to do ventures that I never would have managed without the Cricut, such as making custom names for the majority of my flavor containers — it is extremely unlikely I'd at any point cut those mind boggling letters by hand!

Third, you can make your very own custom tasks. My preferred component of the Cricut Explore is having the option to transfer my very own designs. Nearly all that I make is customized precisely how I need it and it makes all that I make feel considerably more uncommon. You can likewise utilize it to customize gifts — getting a birthday present is extraordinary, yet getting one tweaked with your name is far superior!

Also, fourth, it's not difficult to learn. I figure individuals can be a little overpowered with a machine that accompanies a product they've never utilized. In any case, the Cricut Design Space is easy to use and there are a huge amount of Make It Now extends that have a little expectation to absorb information. Indeed, there are further developed things you can do with the Cricut that will set aside some effort to adapt, yet there are instructional exercises everywhere throughout the Internet on the most proficient method to utilize the machine and the product (counting here on my blog!), and Cricut backing is useful too. If you're terrified of the expectation to absorb information, don't be — simply set aside some effort to become acquainted with the machine and the product, make a couple of basic ventures, and watch YouTube instructional exercises if you're trapped. Try not to give learning the machine a chance to stop you from getting one!

In any case, we should be genuine. In fact practically any undertaking you can do with a Cricut you could without one. Be that as it may, the Cricut will do it So. Much. Better. Your undertakings will look progressively proficient, you'll spare yourself a thousand cerebral pains, you won't squander as much material, and it will be a gobzillion times quicker. I've been making as long as I can remember and this is the primary apparatus that has, and this isn't exaggeration, altered the manner in which I create. It spares personal time, stress, and cash and those things merit everything to me nowadays. I think the Cricut is absolutely justified, despite all the trouble to nearly any individual who wants to create, just as individuals like educators (who need to remove 30 whatevers for their understudies), mothers (who need to customize things for their littles), and even specialists (like model plane developers who need many-sided decals).

REASONS NOT TO BUY A CRICUT

As much as I truly accept that the Cricut is a magnificent making apparatus that you can utilize constantly, I thought of a couple of situations where you should need to hold off getting one. I'm a major adherent to just purchasing what you're going to utilize, and it benefits nobody in any way to have a machine that they never really create with!

In the first place, you must have some craving to be a creator. You could love all the charming things on the planet, however if it's only simpler for you to get it on Etsy because you don't have a craving for making it yourself, your Cricut will sit unused. I do accept that the Cricut makes making and making a whoooole parcel simpler and you don't should be excessively inventive to utilize it since Cricut Access and the Make It Now tasks give you access to such a significant number of extraordinary thoughts. In any case, if you would prefer not to make stuff, you're not really going to make stuff. Am I right?

The second reason you might not have any desire to purchase a Cricut is if you're one of those individuals who simply purchase things because they are cool (indeed, a Cricut is VERY cool). You know your identity! I used to be one of these individuals. I had boxes of cool items, instruments, and supplies that I never utilized. Things sat in boxes and accumulated residue until one day I chose to cleanse everything out of my specialty room that

I didn't effectively utilize. It felt so great however I likewise felt regretful for having so much abundance. Be straightforward with yourself. Regardless of whether you adore the possibility of a Cricut, would you say you are really going to remove it from the container and use it? Is it going to be a piece of your ordinary making day? If in this way, get one. If not, don't squander your cash. A Cricut does nothing simply sitting in a case social occasion dust.

Third is if you extremely simply love cutting stuff by hand. I may believe you're insane and it makes my hands throb simply pondering it — however if that is your thing, put it all on the line!

These reasons are alright! I'd preferably you not feel remorseful for owning a machine that you never use. I'd preferably you spend your cash on something that you will utilize and that will bring you bliss.

Things you Need to Know before Buying one

The Cricut is an extraordinary machine for individuals that affection making, and for or individuals that need to cut a great deal of things and different kinds of materials.

Before I got my Cricut I had TONS and TONS of inquiries. Truth be told! Despite everything I do. That is the reason I am making this monster post so I can archive and spare you the a long stretch of time of research I have done.

In the wake of perusing this incredibly and complete guide you will know if a Cricut Machine is an ideal choice for you!

Is it accurate to say that you are prepared?

This is arrangement of inquiries I had when I purchased my Cricut. I truly wish I approached this kind of substance you are going to peruse. It would've made my life so a lot simpler!

After you are finished perusing this post. You will know without a doubt whether the Cricut is the correct decision for you or not.

These inquiries go from easy to progressively difficult. Subsequently you will gain proficiency with about this machine as you go!

A few inquiries are much increasingly broad and they really require an additional post for it. So if there's a connection to one specific inquiry and you need to get familiar with that subject, simply snap to find out additional.

1. Do I truly require a Cricut?

A Cricut is a cutting machine and is a blessing from heaven for some, crafters out there. You can utilize it for various different things like card making, home stylistic layout, and so forth.

Do you art or wind up in a position where you have to cut a ton? If the response to that is yes. Then you will absolutely profit by having a Cricut. Be that as it may, if you are not into cunning things. Let's be honest! a Cricut isn't something you will truly profit by.

2. Are there different machines that can do something very similar?

Indeed! There are numerous different alternatives you can discover there that can do what the Cricut does to some broaden.

In the market there are two other real brands that likewise cut an extraordinary assortment of materials and that additionally have incredible audits.

These brands are: Silhouette America and Brother.

3. Is the Cricut superior to anything different machines out there?

I accept each bite the dust cutting machine is astounding.

How would I realize that?

It's straightforward. If you take a gander at all of their audits on Amazon you will see that essentially every one of them have multiple begins.

That says that regardless of what machine you pick you will totally adore it

Here's the other thing. Because I happen to have a Cricut and I adore it, I am not going to diss on different brands or machines.

Cricut happens to be the pass on slicing machine brand I chose to go to with. So essentially all you see here will be towards this specific brand

4. For what reason Should I pick Cricut over different brands?

Because it's the one you need.

A few people will say they abhor it, other individuals will say they cherish it. Yet, toward the day's end the cash is leaving your pocket. So you ought to pick what you are progressively OK with.

I for one imagine that Provo Craft and Novelty – the organization that made this stunning instrument – is a slick organization and you can see and feel the nature of their items. You realize that all that they make is made with affection.

Their machines improve inevitably; however they likewise think of new devices and embellishments that make things so a lot simpler and pleasant. You can genuinely grow your breaking points and innovativeness with these machines.

One of different things I have loved about this machine, and that I really discovered after I got it is that the Cricut is in excess of a shaper!

There's the Cricut Community. You can get huge amounts of thoughts and free instructional exercises on the web. We creatives love sharing tips and traps on the best way to exploit this very cool apparatus.

5. For what reason did I get a Cricut?

Not that this inquiry matters to you. In any case, this is the fundamental reason I got one, and you may feel roused by it!

I recall a discussion with my relative where I was asking her what should I blog about. She realizes I make and design beautiful things for basically any event.

In the wake of giving me huge amounts of thoughts; She prescribed me to find out about the Cricut!

The seed was planted. I read huge amounts of instructional exercises, surveys! What's more, a few months after the fact. I GOT ONE!

So for me it was my relative sentiment. She has companions that adoration the machine. So if you know somebody that as of now utilizes a kick the bucket cutting machine and they adore it. Simply take their statement.

Furthermore, if you don't know anybody...

All things considered, Trust me when I state that the Cricut Machine is the best thing out there. You won't be frustrated!

. What are the accessible Cricut Machines out there?

I am going to separate this for you extremely simple! At this moment you there are 3 different models of Cricut Machines accessible:

Cricut Explore Family: These are the most widely recognized machines and they have 3 different alternatives for you to browse. These three machines can cut similar materials, But every one of them have different highlights.

Cricut Explore One: First conceived of the Explore family and just has one apparatus holder so you cut and draw independently.

Cricut Explore Air: Has Bluetooth (This is an absolute necessity for me I don't care for having a string append to my PC) and both device holders so you can cut and draw simultaneously!

Cricut Explore Air 2: Has similar capacities, that the investigate air however it's multiple times quicker.

Cricut Maker: This machine is their most recent discharge and you can cut thick materials like calfskin and even a few kinds of wood.

Cricut Cuttlebug: this is the main Cricut that can formally embellish. Remember that this machine doesn't approach the Cricut Design Space, or any web at all. It's an essential however incredible shaper.

There were different machines accessible also. Furthermore, you may almost certainly buy them on amazon or utilized. Notwithstanding, they are not good with Cricut Design Space and the product they utilized before – Cricut Craft Room – has been closed down totally.

So simply don't purchase any of the old forms. It resembles purchasing a spic and span I-telephone 4. OK do that?

All through this post, except if I notice the Cricut Cuttlebug, most inquiries will be responded in due order regarding the Cricut Explore Family and Cricut Maker.

7. Is the Cricut excessively costly?

Ideal off bat let me reveal to you that YES a Cricut machine can be very costly.

In any case, see I state that it very well may be. This is because if you take a gander at a portion of the primary machines you can see that there are great arrangements and you can begin when you need.

The most affordable machine is the Cricut Cuttlebug – A little however incredible machine – and the Most costly choice is for their most recent discharge, The Cricut Maker.

Look at costs and correlation for the Cricut Explore Family and Cricut Maker

8. Is the Cricut justified, despite all the trouble?

This is so factor and it needs to do about your diversions, needs and furthermore your financial limit.

If you make once per year, listen to me you DON'T require a Cricut. Notwithstanding, if making and making stuff is your jam then a Cricut merits each penny.

You additionally need to see life through your need focal points. For what reason do I say this. Because life is about priorities.\; each choice we make in life ought to be lined up with that.

Is having a Cricut going to profit you and make your life simple enough to spare time – time is cash – and simply make your life progressively charming?

If your answer is YES: Then GO pull the trigger.

I am not the sort of individual that purchases everything. Be that as it may, now and again when I weight upsides and downsides. I simply put it all on the line.

9. What is the best Cricut I can get?

The best Cricut you can get. Pass on is the Cricut Maker.

It's their most up to date discharge and they are concocting numerous devices that will make cutting and making very simple and way progressively pleasant. As it were the Cricut Maker is a definitive Crafter's fantasy.

10. What is the best Cricut for me?

The best Cricut you can get is the one that meets these 3 things:

The one you can bear.

The one you can slice the materials you need to cut.

The one that will leave you with extra cash to purchase materials (regularly overlooked).

This is the reason I got the Air Explore 2 rather than the Cricut Maker.

Most importantly I couldn't bear the cost of the creator. Second of all – as of now in life – I am just keen on cutting paper, vinyl and some texture to a great extent. Furthermore, to wrap things up, what is the purpose of having an increasingly costly machine if you don't have the cash to purchase additional materials to work with?

In any case, if you haven't purchased a machine and you truly need to cut wood and texture I believe is smarter to do the speculation now, and after that get additional apparatuses and materials as you go.

Update: Eventually, I got the Cricut Maker also because I needed to show all of you the conceivable outcomes with the two machines.

11. Would it be a good idea for me to overhaul my Cricut?

If you as of now have a Cricut machine given me a chance to reveal to you something – You ROCK!

Is it true that you are thinking about in updating? I feel you after I purchased my Explore Air 2 I felt deficient, every one of the instructional exercises are currently for the Maker, and that I should simply overhaul.

Isn't that SO SILLY?

Do you redesign your telephone, vehicle, and other electronic gadgets consistently? I sure don't. So – except if I am given one – until I misuse each and every plausibility and I am prepared to learn different strategies. I won't overhaul my machine.

Shouldn't something be said about you?

Would you like to overhaul because you need the most up to date form? Or then again, would you like to update because you really exceeded your present machine?

If you said yes to the second and have the spending limit for it! Welcome to the Cricut Maker family! I am in no uncertainty that you will observe this machine to be an incredible fit for you

12. Where Can I get the Cricut?

There are MANY spots where you can get this machine.

You can think that its essentially at any specialty store like Michael's and JOANN. Indeed, even some Walmart Stores have it accessible. So if you need to begin today you can drive and get it there.

I for one cherish shopping on Cricut's site because that is the place I locate the best arrangements.

13. Does the Cricut and Cricut Materials ever go on Sale?

That's right!

Cricut has things on Sale practically constantly.

You can discover great ones during the occasions and exceptional events. A few retailers additionally run incredible limits. Truth be told I see huge amounts of them on Facebook.

14. Where would i be able to locate the best deals and arrangements for the Cricut?

If I were going to buy a Cricut right now I would do it from their Official Website. They simply have extraordinary limits accessible constantly.

Here you can discover incredible arrangements on packs, machines, and materials.

15. What materials would i be able to cut with the Cricut?

There are hundreds – actually – of materials you can cut with these astonishing machine these are some of them:

Plan Paper

A wide range of cardstock

Metallic Paper

Vinyl (Iron on, sparkle, lasting, removable)

Texture and materials

Artificial Leather

Ridged Paper

Meager Woods (Cricut Maker as it were)

Sticker Paper

Material Paper

And the sky is the limit from there!

16. Where would i be able to get Cricut materials?

You can get materials in your preferred Craft Store. Much the same as you would get the Cricut.

I am truly astonished at all of the alternatives you can discover on the web. Amazon has hundreds if not a great many choices for you to buy.

The Cricut site likewise has cool materials, yet they just offer their very own image. Be that as it may, my preferred spot to get materials is Michaels; I adore strolling through the isles, I can truly invests huge amounts of energy (and cash ahhg) there.

17. Are Cricut materials costly?

Contingent upon the undertakings you need to cut, Cricut Materials can be very costly. This is the reason you should buy the machine that will likewise enable you to purchase things to cut.

It's silly for you to get the Cricut Maker if you wont have an additional spending limit for you to cut different materials. That resembles purchasing Snow Tires when you live in Florida, and there's no Snow. Get my point?

Easily overlooked details to a great extent, truly include. Materials like basswood can be over the top expensive too.

At the present time, I am concentrating more on paper, and I will move my way up. Paper is the most ideal route for you to gain proficiency with your machine because if you cut something incorrectly is simply paper. So it is anything but a major ordeal if you mess it up.

18. Would i be able to use off brand materials to use with my Cricut?

Truly, indeed, yes!

You don't need to be constrained to the materials that Cricut makes. There are hundreds if not a large number of astonishing materials you can get on the web or on your preferred Craft store.

I am certain that with time there will be considerably more alternatives.

19. What is the Cricut riddle box and how can it work?

Consistently Cricut discharges a Mystery Box!

This container is load up with astonishing materials yet you truly don't have the foggiest idea what they are. It's an amazement till you get that crate!

The astounding thing about this crate is that you will get more than what you really paid. What I mean by this is if you were going to purchase the majority of the materials that come in the crate independently the cost would be so a lot higher.

They do run out. So try to get yours toward the start of every month!

20. What is the Cricut versatile device System?

The Cricut Adaptive System is an amazingly and ground-breaking highlight that lone the Cricut Maker has. This element controls the heading and of the edge at untouched. Actually, This apparatus is stunning to the point that it can modify the weight of the cutting edge to coordinate the materials you are working with!

This innovation is the thing that enables the Cricut Maker to cut with 10X more power than any of the other Cricut Explore Family machines.

This is the reason the Maker can cut thick materials like wood and cowhide.

Cool. Isn't that so?

21. Does the Cricut print?

The Cricut Machine doesn't print. Be that as it may, the majority of the present machines they offer – Except Cuttlebug – have a choice to draw and diagram things like letters, shapes, and so on.

If you as of now have a Cricut, this inquiry appears to be so self-evident. Be that as it may, I had this inquiry before I purchased mine. What's more, I genuinely couldn't locate a reasonable response to it.

22. Does the Cricut need ink?

You needn't bother with ink to utilize your Cricut. Because it doesn't print.

Be that as it may, if you are going to utilize the illustration choice. you need their pens so as to have the option to draw. They have an extraordinary assortment of alternatives for you to look over.

23. Does the Cricut Laminate?

No. The Cricut Machines don't overlay. Wouldn't it be decent, however?

24. Does the Cricut Emboss?

The main Cricut Machine that can really decorate is the Cricut Cuttlebug.

This is the thing that the official site says: "The main Cricut® machine that can embellish, the Cricut Cuttlebug™gives proficient looking outcomes with spotless, fresh cuts and profound, even decorates."

Be that as it may, you can discover workarounds and make stencils with any of different machines and decorate essentially anything your heart wants. While I was examining this inquiry, I discovered huge amounts of cool instructional exercises on YouTube that show you how to do it! This was my top choice.

25. Does the Cricut Sew?

No. The Cricut doesn't sew. It's so natural to feel that it does because you hear the majority of the beneficial things that you can do if you are a sewer.

26. Does the Cricut cut texture?

Truly, the Cricut can cut texture.

If you work with textures and need to cut huge amounts of texture in different sizes, the Cricut will be your best and increasingly confided in Cutting partner.

The Cricut producer enables you to cut texture with no fortified material. Along these lines, if sewing is your calling and this is the principle explanation behind you to get a Cricut. I will very prescribe to put resources into the Maker.

You can cut Fabric with the Any of the Cricut Explore Family machines. Notwithstanding, the texture should be reinforced. I will clarify better in the following inquiry.

27. What on the planet is a support material, and how can it identify with cutting texture?

Would you be able to trust I couldn't locate an average response to this? Fortunately, I am here to clarify you what this implies

The Cricut Explore Family machines and the Cricut Maker can cut texture. Be that as it may, there's a major proviso and that will be that with the end goal for you to have the option to cut texture with the Explore Family machines you need a support material.

Support – or otherwise called Heat and Bond – in the Cricut and pass on cutting machines world is a sort of material that enables you to settle textures on the cutting mat. As such, If you don't hold fast this material to your textures when utilizing the Cricut Explore Machines, your textures won't get cut up appropriately, and they will get destroyed and additionally extended.

Dreadful right?

28. Does the Cricut cut wood?

Truly and No. Out of all the cutting machines that Cricut has accessible. Just the Cricut Maker can cut wood. A portion of the kinds of wood you can cut are balsa and basswood.

You likewise need to remember that the Cricut Maker itself with the typical cutting edge that accompanies DOES NOT cut wood. For these sort of task, you will require the Knife Blade, which is a sort cutting edge that is specifically designed to cut thick materials.

29. What are a portion of the undertakings I can do with a Cricut Machine?

There are numerous activities you can make with a Cricut machine! This is only a modest rundown of a portion of the things you can achieve. Note: Links on this area are a portion of my Cricut instructional exercises.

Home Decoration: Decals for your windows, dividers. Or on the other hand, something that I like a great deal is to customize things like crates, or even your cooking flavors.

Stickers: for arranging, journaling, and that's only the tip of the iceberg

Welcome Cards: You can make top of the line welcome cards. Like those, you find in the store!

Garments Items: Cut and iron on beautiful and customized designs on your T-Shirts.

3D Projects: like gift boxes and even paper toys! –

With the Cricut Maker, you can cut wood and make 3D and tough ventures.

Cut texture and make design things for your dress and the sky is the limit from there.

Your creative mind is the utmost!

30. What on the planet are Cricut cartridges and Do I need them?

The word cartridge in the Cricut world is different than in the printing scene; I feel that is the reason I figured the Cricut could print!

Fundamentally Cricut Cartridges are a lot of pictures, designs or textual styles you can buy and get the chance to keep until the end of time. They are normally designed around a specific subject, for example, Disney, Pop Corn gathering, and anything you can essentially consider.

There are 2 kinds of cartridges. Physical and Digital, the physical ones can be embedded in the machine. Also, the Digital ones you can legitimately buy from the Cricut site or Cricut Design Space.

When you initiate the cartridges, they will be accessible to you on the product, and the physical variants are never again required.

I get the inclination that the Physical Cartridges will be ceased sooner or later. A major confirmation of this is the Cricut Maker – their most recent discharge – doesn't have a space for you to embed them. (You have to purchase a connector for this)

31. What is Cricut Infusible Ink?

Cricut Infusible Ink is a sort of innovation that permits to you make and move your designs to a base material. What makes this innovation so interesting is that the Infusible Ink move will end up one with the base material you pick.

The outcomes in the wake of applying Cricut Infusible ink are stunning and amazingly high caliber. They are consistently smooth, don't ring endlessly, and they will remain in your base material until the end of time.

32. What on the planet are Cricut Mats and which one do I need?

You have no clue the majority of the migraines I got attempting to make sense of this!

A Cricut Mat is the surface you use with the goal for you to have the option to cut specific materials. They come in 2 different sizes: 12 x 12 and 12 x 24 inches.

The Cricut Mats are sticky and depending of the material you are going to cut you are in an ideal situation utilizing different degrees of stickiness. Or then again otherwise called a holds.

As of now there are 4 sorts of mats:

Light Grip (Blue)

Solid Grip (Purple)

Standard Grip (Green)

Texture Grip (Pink)

When I initially got my Cricut, I got a pleasant pack on Amazon that incorporated the 4 mats.

If you are simply beginning. The best MAT for you is the standard grasp. The more grounded the hold, the heavier the material you can utilize.

For example it you are cutting ordinary and dainty paper you would utilize a Light Grip tangle, however, if you are anticipating cutting a heavier material like thick Cardstock you are in an ideal situation with a Strong Grip tangle.

Essentially every machine accompanies a Standard Grip Mat. Ensure you read the portrayal of the items before you purchase.

If you need to adapt more top to bottom about Cricut Mats make a point to peruse this book. It will indicate you all that you have to know.

33. What is a Cricut Blade and which one do I need?

The cutting edge is the thing that cuts the materials. lol Right?

Be that as it may, there's something significant for you to know, before you begin and if you are anticipating cutting thicker materials

Right now there are 5 cutting edges accessible. Every sharp edge has different capacities and is fit to cut different materials.

Fine Point Blade: Ideal for light and medium materials like paper, vinyl and cardstock. It comes now in a gold shading.

Profound Point Blade: Great for thick materials like chipboard, thick cardstock, froth sheets, and so forth.

Fortified Fabric Blade: Ideal for cutting texture! Texture should be fortified with support material.

Revolving Blade (Only for the Cricut Maker): Cuts practically any kind of texture and the texture can be simply place on the tangle. It accompanies the Maker and at the minutes it's not sold separately. Be that as it may, they do sell the revolving substitution unit

Knife Blade (Only for the Cricut Maker): This great little edge can cut exceptionally thick materials like basswood!

So if wood is your jam, then the Cricut Maker + the Knife cutting edge are an unquestionable requirement.

If you need to become familiar with the majority of the Cricut Blades and their differences, read this extreme guide

34. What edges accompany each Cricut Machine?

When you purchase only a machine (No pack) the generally accompany a cutting edge. How about we see what cutting edge accompanies each machine!

Cricut Explore One: fine point cutting edge

Cricut Explore Air: fine point edge

Cricut Explore Air 2: fine point sharp edge

Cricut Maker: Rotary sharp edge, fine point cutting edge

35. To what extent does the Cricut Blade Last?

Cricut Blades keep going relying upon the material and recurrence you use them.

There's not by any stretch of the imagination a specific time for it. If you see your materials aren't being cut with a similar freshness and facilitate that they used to. Then it's the ideal opportunity for you to supplant it.

36. What Other Cricut Accessories do I need?

This is a dubious inquiry, and It thoroughly relies upon the sort of materials you need to work with and cut.

Despite the fact that the Cricut machines are equipped for some things, you have to utilize it with the correct apparatuses to genuinely make it work. For example, if you have any of the Explore Family Machines and need to cut texture, you have to ensure that you have:

Sponsorship Material

Texture Bonded – Blade

Standard Grip Mat

Then again if you need to cut texture with the creator you can likewise utilize the above apparatus, or you can pick a rotating sharp edge in addition to a Fabric Grip Mat.

Most normal and light weight materials can be cut with the Fine Point Blade (The cutting edge that accompanies each machine) and the Standard grasp Mat.

Be that as it may, as you investigate and become increasingly mindful of your machine and the materials you are utilizing, things will turn out to be a great deal more simpler!

I know it's precarious however once you get the hang of it you will be a specialist. The beneficial thing about this machine is that when you are going to cut a specific material, the program will let you know precisely what materials you need!

Cool right?

Another significant thing here and something that I consider critical is to get is a portion of the their extraordinary devices.

There are various sets for you to look over. Be that as it may, the most well-known are the Basic, and the Essential Tool set.

37. Is it better for me to get a pack or simply the machine?

If you visit the Cricut Online Store, Amazon, and other online retailers you will see that there huge amounts of packs you can buy.

I really got a group myself from Amazon. They are great worth and accompanied a beginning pack for you to begin as quickly as time permits.

When you are searching for packs, ensure they incorporate what you need to begin with.

For example, if you are simply going to begin cutting vinyl and paper. The ideal pack for you will incorporate your preferred machine + some vinyl sheets + standard grasp tangle + essential toolbox. (This is the thing that I got)

Nonetheless, if your fundamental intention is to cut texture. You need a pack that accompanies the fundamentals for you to begin. Like sewing instruments and so on.

If you get the Cricut Maker they have extraordinary choices for you to begin cutting texture.

38. Is there something different I need other than the Cricut and Accessories:

There are different things you need and there are regularly not referenced:

Materials you need to cut and learn with. I will prescribe you to rehearse with paper tons and tons before you choose to cut something like texture or wood that can be increasingly costly.

Persistence: It's an expectation to learn and adapt... Not all things will come simple, however will turn out to be simple

YouTube gorge instructional exercises for you to totally ace this machine – I am anticipating putting TONS of stunning instructional exercises. If you like this post make a point to buy in (It's likewise an incredible manner to help my work)

39. What on the planet is a Cricut Easy Press?

A Cricut Easy Press is a cool gadget that permits you move your Iron On vinyl to T-shirts, sweaters, blankets and that's just the beginning! It comes in 3 different sizes and you can get the one that addresses your issues:

The sizes are:

9×9 Inches: This size is incredible to move designs to Adult size T-Shirts

6×7 Inches: Ideal to press on little bits of dress like onesies and other infant garments.

10×12 Inches: Perfect to Iron on in enormous surfaces like blankets and covers.

40. Is the Cricut Easy Press extremely justified, despite all the trouble?

This is a Yes and No answer, for me the appropriate response tilts more to the no extremely justified, despite all the trouble.

The principle reason is because I can simply utilize my customary iron; and since I am not completing a great deal of iron on activities right now It doesn't generally bode well for me to contribute on it.

41. Is the Cricut simple to utilize?

Everything in life has an expectation to learn and adapt.

When my Cricut arrived I felt a smidgen overpowered I admit! It very well may threaten from the start, yet once you get its hang. I am certain those staggering days will be only relics of days gone by.

So the principle believe is to stay with it. Watch the same number of YouTube channels (I am making my own) and Instagram recordings you can. Search for instructional exercises! I will put EVERYTHING you have to know. No doubt

Try not to overwhelm... . We are in the data age, and information is earnestly at the tip of a google search.

42. Do I should be a technically knowledgeable to have the option to utilize the Cricut?

You don't should be super, technically knowledgeable. Anyway, you do need to know a few nuts and bolts and fundamentals about the manner in which the PCs work. For example, you have to realize how to function PCs a tad. Things

Like opening a page and login into Cricut Design Space – Where you organize the thing you have to cut.

If you have a Smart telephone and need to work your machine inside the application. You likewise should be natural on the most proficient method to download the application.

Do you believe you won't most likely learn it? Try not to feel like that! The sky is the limit if you put the time and exertion.

I am here perking you up. Additionally, I have the majority of the aim of making this learning open to you!

43. What is the Cricut perfect with?

All together for your machine to work, you should be associated with the Cricut Design Space.

The Cricut Design Space is just perfect with Windows and Mac working frameworks. At the end of the day; you need a personal computer with the end goal for you to utilize the Cricut Machines.

If you need to utilize your machine without web, you have to download the Cricut Design Space application. This application is very helpful, and it interface by means of Bluetooth.

This application is accessible just for iOS a.k.a Iphone and Apple clients.

In any case, if you are an Android client, don't lose trust! Cricut just discharged a beta alternative and in spite of the fact that It doesn't have every one of the abilities you would have on an Iphone. I am almost certain one day it will arrive.

44. Would i be able to associate my Cricut by means of Bluetooth to my telephone or PC?

It relies upon the machine you have.

The Explore Air, Explore Air 2, and Maker have worked in Bluetooth innovation so they can associate with your work area or telephone.

For the Cricut Explore One you will require a connector to have the option to interface your Cricut through Bluetooth to your PC or telephone. If you as of now have this machine I believe is something great to have.

In any case, if you're simply inquiring about what machine is ideal, I would recommend to begin looking from the Explore Air or more.

NOTE: The Cricut Cuttlebug doesn't have any electronic or Bluetooth abilities.

45. Do I need Internet for me to utilize the Cricut?

If you are wanting to utilize your Cricut from your PC, you NEED to have Internet get to. Notwithstanding, the Cricut

Design App – Available for iOS and Android telephones – will permit to utilize your Cricut machine disconnected.

46. Is there an elective Software to utilize the Cricut?

Probably not!

Obviously, there was a path for you to do it with an outsider program; however, it's not accessible with the fresher machines.

What I for one do is that I design what I have to Cut on Illustrator, and afterward I cut it on my printer. In any case, if it's simply content and essential shapes. The Cricut Design Space is simply enough.

47. How does the Cricut work?

So far you've found out about the Cricut itself. Things like the mats, cutting edges, materials, and what the machines are perfect with.

However, how does the Cricut really work? For the Cricut Machine to cut, you have to utilize it alongside the Cricut Design Space. This is where you'll lay and sort out your design to be cut.

48. What is Cricut Design Space?

The Cricut Design Space is the product that enables you to compose, make, lastly cut your undertakings. Without the Design Space you can't work your machine. That is for what reason is significant for you to figure out how to utilize it.

The Cricut Machine is extraordinary yet if you don't figure out how to utilize the Design Space, it resembles purchasing a camera and not taking photographs. Or then again purchasing a Smart Phone and not making a telephone or video call.

49. Is Cricut Design Space Free?

Indeed!

All things considered, if you have machine is free

You can transfer your very own designs to be cut. You can even access your framework's textual styles and a few shapes to make straightforward cuts for nothing.

What's not free is Cricut Access.

50. What is Cricut Access?

Cricut Access is a GIANT library that will enable you to choose and make officially designed activities. This is helpful it you are simply beginning.

When you have Cricut Access and relying upon the arrangement you have, you can choose one of a kind text styles, illustrations, 3D Projects, and if you can think it, they have it.

They have ventures for any event and any materials you like to work with. It's very great.

CONCLUSION

The Cricut cutting machine is as astonishing as it is because of Cricut Design Space, the free application that causes the enchantment to occur. And keeping in mind that Cricut Design Space is entirely simple and easy to use, acing it doesn't occur without any forethought.

That is for what reason I'm here to share my most loved Cricut Design Space instructional exercises, tips, and traps with you! These will change your Cricut life!

Made in the USA
Columbia, SC
12 December 2020